START WITH ONE

To all those that I've had the great opportunity to teach, train, lead, guide, and learn from- thank you for showing me that a little momentum can move mountains.

To my friends, family, and "sistas", I love you and am so grateful for you in my life! To everyone that helped me bring this book into being — Heather, Michelle, Amanda, Josie, Jeff, and the EPIC team, Thank you!

Thank you to my husband, Lance, for being my best life partner and for always loving me as I am. And finally, I thank my Creator whose light and love guides my days and gives me breath.

START with ONE

A Simple Approach to Upgrade Your Health - Body, Mind, & Spirit

by
Kathleen Klug

Contents

Introduction

Holistic Health, also referred to as Integrated Health, is a way of looking at the whole health of who we are as humans – connected in body, mind, and spirit. My goal in writing *START with ONE* is to help you identify what holistic and healthy integrated health means to you, to give you guidance to identify where you are and where you want to be, then to give you tools and skills to develop and to create it. This book shows you how to eat healthier, move more, think higher, and love better by identifying small but significant ways to start a shift, a movement, a momentum, to positive and integrated health.

I'll start by showing you the importance of the body, mind, and spirit integration to health and wellness. Then we'll explore ways to improve your health, including identifying good nutrition to nourish your body, building a healthy movement habit, bringing awareness and intention to affirming thoughts to bring up your vibe, and nurturing your soul.

My hope is that as you read this book, you'll feel empowered knowing that you can, and in fact you are the only one who can, choose your behavior and change your health. That you can get healthier, stronger, fitter, freer, and happier, if you so choose. This work we do, and the journey it takes us on, is an inside job - one that starts with desire and decision, and moves into action with a plan. And always, this journey is covered with kindness, grace, and acceptance. The journey is never about perfection, but rather the becoming and unfolding of your best self, with love.

I often hear people who feel frustrated or overwhelmed at the state they are in, but they also feel frozen in anxiety or panic because the task before them to change their situation, as they perceive it (health, job, relationship, etc.), seems too enormous and they don't know where to start. Or they think there is no way to get all the way over *there* so they don't do anything. Because we are integrated (connected) beings, when we improve in one area of our life, the other areas can and will improve as well. And doing ONE thing differently with your body, mind, or in your spirit, has the power to bring momentum, energy, and self-empowerment that can change your health.

The structure that *START with ONE* will walk you through is the *HOW-TO* to identify ONE achievable target behavior to begin with in any area of your life that you want to improve. No matter your goal – whether you want to improve physically, mentally and emotionally, or spiritually - you will have the tools, structure, understanding, and support to improve, restore, and integrate your health and create more energy, joy, and purpose in your life!

When you have health - true integrated health - you can create and do just about anything! Having this kind of health is everything, and you are the one that must take charge of your health. Be your own champion in your own life and START with ONE, right now!

Part I

WE ARE INTEGRATED BEINGS

CHAPTER ONE

Integrated Health - Body, Mind, and Spirit

"Natural forces within us are the true healers of disease."
Hippocrates

What is integrated health? It is the connectivity, harmony, and health of our body, mind, and spirit. It is the recognition that what we do, think, feel, and believe in, influences our ability to heal, and informs our mood, energy, actions, and our sense of hope and purpose. Hippocrates (460 BCE), known as the Father of Medicine, understood the power of integration in healing medicine, and believed that our bodies had natural forces within, or rather natural innate abilities, to overcome disease, including, and possibly most especially, the power of a person's frame of mind and perception of their illness to predict their treatment success and cure rate.

This is why, when we talk about integrated health, we must consider everything that makes *US* who we are, if we want true, integrated, and whole health. This means considering everything put in and on the body, as well as what is allowed into the mind and spirit. It isn't possible to separate the different parts of us like they exist without connection or dependence on the other parts. What you want to do is become aware of, and strive for, good, positive, high vibe nourishment for healthy integration.

Today there is more and more talk and awareness around integrated health and holistic health care and treatment. We see integrated health care gaining more attention through the practices of Functional Medicine, Holistic Medicine, Osteopathic Medicine, Ayurvedic Medicine, and Integrated Health Coaches & Practitioners. These integrative approaches consider the whole person - body, mind, and spirit - and are growing and educating people that putting a Band-Aid on their physical or emotional symptoms or giving out pills to "treat" an ailment, does not make their troubles go away. Instead, this more integrated approach considers food, movement, social connection, sleep patterns, sense of purpose, relationships, home environment, gut health, allergies, belief systems, and the quality of thought patterns.

Because we are integrated beings, we cannot separate the body from the mind or the spirit because what affects one, affects the other. The food we eat and our movement, or lack of, affects the mind as well as our emotions, and this affects the spirit. What we think, believe, and act upon affect our bodies, minds, and spirits, and are displayed in the way we make choices, and our lives are witness to those choices. Our spirit and sense of purpose, connection, and love, for example, feed our emotional and thinking minds, as well as communicate with every cell in our body, and inform them how to respond at a cellular level.

We know that one can eat healthy foods, get more than enough exercise and, by the looks of it, appear healthy, but still be stuck in illness or disease. Unresolved pain, unforgiveness, negative sense of self, lack of purpose, belief of unworthiness, bitterness, regret, guilt, fear, and worry - all the beliefs and thoughts that keep us in these toxic emotions, also keep our body in a toxic state and keep us from true health and healing. Chemicals, such as the stress hormones cortisol, adrenaline, and epinephrine are released into our blood and body when we think fearful, negative thoughts. When we experience the connected emotions with these thoughts, it compromises our ability to be well and stresses our immune function, which can bring disease no matter how many vegetables you consume, or how many miles you run. The constant production and flood of these neurochemicals in our body are linked to heart disease, high blood sugar, high blood pressure, suppressed immunity, obesity, digestive issues, depression and chronic illness.

The contrary is also true. Positive thoughts charged with strong, positive emotions - love, joy, and gratitude, for example, release happy neurochemicals such as dopamine, serotonin, and oxytocin. These neurochemicals have power to heal and restore our bodies into health on a cellular level. Consider a study done by Northwestern Medicine neurologist, Danny Bega, MD, where they treated patients with Parkinson's Disease with laughter. The laughter treatment demonstrated improvement in non-motor skills as well as enhanced, meaningful quality of life. [1]The small and simple act of laughing benefits the body, mind, and spirit in many ways: reduces stress, boosts the immune system, regulates blood pressure, improves pain tolerance, and improves brain function and memory.

These points are stated to help you better understand the link between the physical world of your body, and the unseen world of your psyche and spirit, and to acknowledge the fact that we are interwoven and designed to be integrated in body, mind, and spirit.

---

[1] Laughter is the best medicine: The Second City improvisation as an intervention for Parkinson's disease. Danny Bega, et.al. Published: November 2016

CHAPTER TWO

START with ONE

"The Journey of a Thousand Miles starts with one Step."
Lao Tzu

I've heard it said that the first step is always the hardest. You may relate to this. Why do you think that is? It may be because we don't know what the second step will look like, or if we'll know how to proceed as we go along. So for many of us, we don't start with the first step because we don't know the what or the how of the second step. Or, it could be we do know, or think we know, and we are afraid of the (possible) outcome, so we don't start. It may also be that it's because we have tried before and failed, and we don't want to experience that failure again, believing we can't do it differently this time. Feeling fearful and doubtful to try again at something that you started before and that you failed at, is normal. (I don't even like the word "failed" because it implies a total loss, a big zero, or a complete loser, but I see failure as an opportunity to learn about oneself, to identify weaknesses that need support, and a chance to learn what works and what doesn't work.) In my work as a Health Educator, I see participants so overwhelmed with lack of confidence and fear, that they can be on the verge of quitting on themselves and the program everyday because their internal negative voice regularly reminds them of their past failures, especially when they feel the most vulnerable. They want so desperately to change, but their lack of confidence and the fear of another disappointment terrifies them. I applaud them for their courage to show up and start with their first step. It really doesn't have to be difficult if one had a plan that is so doable, that it would actually be hard to fail. My message to the people I have worked with over the years has been - START with ONE. Just find one simple thing to do differently and become consistent at it. Whether the goal is to:

1) Lose weight	4) Get in shape	6) Laugh more
2) Clean up your home	Eat better	Help the environment
Improve relationships	Find greater purpose	Find greater joy
3) Enhance your career	Get connected with others	5) Go after your dream
Be more active	Serve more	Find a soul partner
Heal past wounds	Create more	Find yourself

No matter the goal, they all really do START with ONE step - the first one. The truth of this is already very well known to you and you've been doing this all your life, whether consciously or unconsciously. As a baby you followed this rule when you first rolled over, then crawled, walked, and soon after, ran. You finished school by attending one day at a time, one class at a time, one year at a time. A person who loses 100 pounds, does so 1 pound at a time. Someone who saves $1,000, does so $1 at a time. This book was written one page and one idea at a time. Dreams and desires are created and come to life by a decision, a plan, and then one action at a time.

Your physical, mental, and spiritual health is where it is because of your small, consistent behaviors that have added up. Your life reflects the beliefs, thoughts, and feelings you have been nourishing for years, for better or worse. The empowerment of START with ONE is that any one alive and breathing can, and is

10

already doing this in one direction or the other. No special talent, education, or intelligence is required. The only thing you need to start is knowing where you want to go, or at the very least, the direction you want to go towards.

Here is an example of the power of START with ONE:

You are in the habit of eating too much unhealthy food. You want to lose weight, and you have tried "every" diet out there. You've lost weight only to regain it back because your new way of eating either wasn't sustainable, or your old habits came flooding back. Before you know it, you are doing what you always did and ended up back where you were - at your starting weight, or even more this time.

Damn though. You were so excited and optimistic, and now look! Another failed attempt. This up and down can leave one feeling fearful and doubtful that they can actually change.

So where do you start? How do you do it differently this time?

In this example, you can consider ONE small change in your diet, such as a decision to drink more water. It may seem like an insignificant thing considering what you want and need to change, but just hang with me here. Maybe you are drinking 10 ounces of water a day. You are also drinking 3 diet sodas, 4 cups of coffee and 2 glasses of wine every day. If a commitment and plan was made to drink the minimum RDA of 64 ounces a day, that extra 54 ounces of water may take the place of a few sodas or other beverages simply because you are more full from the water and simply don't have room for your normal soda/coffee/wine intake (the crowd out effect).

The additional water could help you experience increased energy and reduced fatigue that would help with your ability to think and focus. Your increased water intake could improve your skin complexion, promote weight loss, help flush out toxins from your body, support regularity, aid in digestion, aid in normalizing blood pressure, and more. This ONE thing would help you feel better, and quickly. The focus was not on eliminating the sodas, coffee, alcohol, or even making any changes to your food (yet), it was only on drinking 64 ounces of water a day. That ONE thing made a difference. It also started an idea that if you can do that, then you can do another ONE thing. Maybe the next ONE thing is to add 1 or 2 more servings of vegetables into your daily food intake. There again you would feel almost immediate benefits with small, doable, consistent behaviors that have a quick return.

The same idea would be true to clear out the stuck energy of unresolved anger or bitterness. You could make a commitment to say ONE prayer a day for the person you hold resentment against. That one prayer (this could even be a one-minute prayer!) done consistently has the power to loosen the grip on the bitterness that binds you, or open even a crack for softness to come into your heart. To progress this, you may commit to sit quietly for 5 minutes a day and connect with the things in life that you are grateful for. Done consistently, our bodies respond to gratitude at a cellular level with chemicals that create an environment for healing and restoration. [2] With more deliberate gratitude in your body, mind, and spirit, you will likely experience more joy and energy.

I worked with a gal who experienced the momentum of change by starting with one very simple and small action - a few cups of water. We started working together because she knew her lifestyle was making her sick and she didn't want to keep going in this direction. This bright and intelligent woman ran her business from her computer at home, where she would sit for hours and hours everyday, feeling overwhelming stress from her responsibilities and workload. She was

---

[2] Gratitude is good medicine. Practicing gratitude boosts emotional and physical wellbeing. UC Davis Health. November 25, 2015

eating poorly, chronically dehydrated, sitting all day, and feeling tense, strained and anxious much of the day and night. Her body, mind, and spirit were suffering - her back and neck hurt, she was gaining weight, she wasn't sleeping well, she had chronic fatigue, her marriage was neglected, and she felt like she was aging at an exponential rate.

Adding anything more than one small simple step to her life would have felt like an overload to her, so we started very small: drink 4 glasses of water throughout your day. Fill up your water bottle in the morning, set it on your desk, set your phone alarm and when it goes off, drink your water. Sounds simple enough, right? Well, she was used to working without stopping. She would sit and work through her body calling her to action. She would ignore her need for water, need to pee, need to eat (although when she did finally stop to eat, she would binge eat because she was so hungry and depleted) and her aching back. She had conditioned herself to "snooze the alarm" when her body called. And she did the same thing with the new water alarm at first - she snoozed it, then snoozed it again. She had to become aware of, and commit to not snoozing her alarm on her one small step - drinking her water. And she did.

Soon she was drinking 8 to 9 glasses of water a day. We then had her get up from her desk to drink her water - she used her alarm system to alert her it was time, and she committed to get up, walk into the kitchen and drink a glass of water when her alarm went off. She was allowing the alarm to trigger her to STOP, get up, and hydrate. This served to get her out of her desk, even for a few minutes, drink some water, take a pee, and this gave her a mini mental reset as well.

These small simple steps continued to move her into other small simple steps. She would get up during her morning mini breaks to drink water and prepare a healthy snack. Her mid-day mini break now prompted her to take the dog out for a 20-30 minute walk during her newly designated lunch time. She started planning and prepping a healthy lunch the night before. And, she found a walking partner to walk around the neighborhood after work with. This prompted her to close down her computer at a designated time as well.

Her body was feeling better because it was hydrated and fueled better, plus her new movement throughout the day was bringing in feel-good neurochemicals that gave her a new perspective of balance in her life. That taking care of herself made her **want to** move. It made her want to be a nicer person to her husband, a less stressed out business owner, and a healthier person who looks and feels good.

Today, she is a different person than the one I first met. She continues to identify ways she can make one small change to keep moving her in an even healthier direction. She told me at first the small changes were challenging, but she recognized that it was because of her perceived overwhelm and complete lack of balance and self-care. Once she began with the smallest of steps - adding the water, she almost immediately felt a shift and momentum that she could make healthy changes. Her mindset changed and her confidence grew, and with that, the small changes became easy and so rewarding. But it all started with a few glasses of water.

These small, simple steps start a movement in the body towards health, and with awareness, desire, and a plan for better and more integrated health, you would easily be able to continue with ONE small behavior. And done consistently, these small behaviors create healing in your body, mind, and spirit. Behavior and action add up - even the smallest of actions, done consistently, over time, can create big changes. What if you added even one of any of these small actions for a week, month, or twelve months? How could your life be different? Do you think this one small action would lead you to another small action, and so on and so on?

Consider one small action everyday: add one vegetable; one call, one walk, one 1:00 minute meditation, one apple, one hug, one "I love you", one compliment, one prayer, one forgiveness, one page, one 'pay-it-forward', one encouragement.

Or one small action once a week: try a new recipe, taste a new food, have a hearty laugh, make a meal for someone, help someone with a need, write a letter, do a weight workout, take a bath, connect with a friend, buy a stranger a coffee, go dancing, take a yoga class, play a game.

And what if you consistently on a monthly basis: saved $100, explored a new hike, restaurant, winery, or sporting event, or went on a getaway with your honey, read a book, did a home project, or volunteered and served others?

If you decided and acted with one action consistently, you would look back in a week, month, or year and be proud and amazed at what you accomplished, and you would realize that it wasn't so difficult. The consistency of the smallest of actions keeps this kind of progress so very doable!

In this book, I am going to show you how to START with ONE. No matter where you start, no matter how small a change you make, if done consistently, over time, you can make a difference in your life. That difference will change you in your body, mind, and spirit. The fact that we are never just staying still in one place indicates that we are either making headway in one direction or the other as the basic law of "Create or Disintegrate" is at work, always. So the question is, which direction will you move towards?

"For time and the world do not stand still.
Change is the law of life."
John F. Kennedy

15

Part II

THE STATE OF YOUR HEALTH

CHAPTER THREE

The Standard American Food Trap

How did you get to where you are at this moment? Here you will look at the different areas of health and the possible ways you arrived where you are today. In this chapter, we'll look at the state of your physical body and the specific influence of our diet on our health. To start with, take a good, hard, honest look at your physical health and how you feel about where you are. Ask yourself the following questions and answer "yes" or "no" for each one:

PERSONAL HEALTH ASSESSMENT	Y	N
Am I happy with my physical health?	✓	
Do I regularly exercise?	✓	
Am I in a healthy weight range for my body height and age?	✓	
Do I have good energy for the things that I want to do?	✓	
Does my diet consist mostly of whole and healthy foods?	✓	
Do I have good heart and blood health?	✓	
Do I have good strength, flexibility, agility, and stamina to enjoy life's offerings?	✓	
Do I get enough quality sleep to rejuvenate properly?	✓	
Do I take minimal or no medications?	✓	
Do I feel healthy?	✓	

"You're too good to feel this bad."
Dr. Nate Dallas

If you said yes to many or all of these questions, it is because you have been creating this physical state with good food choices, activity, and other lifestyle choices that have resulted in good physical health.

If you are not in a place where you are saying yes to these questions, it, too, is because you have been creating this physical state with your behaviors, choices, and habits, albeit different ones.

If you are experiencing a chronic health condition or disorder, a habitual or addictive relationship with drugs or alcohol, feel stress or anxiety on a regular basis, lack strength and stamina, or you generally feel too tired or too foggy to show up in your life the way that you would like to show up, read on and see if you can identify possible causes or symptoms that relate to how you feel. The first way we tackle any change is by becoming aware of what we are dealing with.

Just to be clear, I am not talking about needing to have a lean, mean, fighting machine of a body when I speak of good physical health. I am speaking of the ability to live the life that you want to - whether it be to walk, garden, play with your kids or grandkids, ski, travel, explore nature, think clearly, create, and simply be present in your life, with intention. This kind of physical health is accessible to just about everyone, regardless of age, or even other physical limitations.

I understand there may be many people reading this who are in the middle of disease, illness, or disability, but regardless of where you are currently with your body, what we know for sure is that eating healthy, whole foods, moving your body, getting adequate sleep, and learning to manage stress will move you in the direction of better health. That is simply a fact.

Let's look at food first.

The role of food in our integrated health: I believe we all know what food is, but this is the definition according to Brittanica:

Food: *substance consisting essentially of protein, carbohydrate, fat, and other nutrients used in the body of an organism to sustain growth and vital processes and to furnish energy.* [3]

This is an important definition because we think food is everything we see at the grocery store and it simply is not if we consider this definition: " ...to sustain growth and vital processes..". It is estimated that the average grocery store will carry over 40,000 products, half of those items are food products. I don't know the percentage of foods on the shelves that would not meet the definition of food in respect to "sustain growth and vital processes" but I believe it is a large percentage. Consider:

- *A study from the American Journal of Clinical Nutrition has found that almost two-thirds — 60 percent — of American grocery purchases are highly processed foods. In addition, 77 percent of American grocery purchases consist of either moderately or highly processed foods.*[4]
- *Per the World Health Organization (WHO), 80%+ of deaths from heart disease and stroke are caused by high blood pressure, tobacco use, elevated cholesterol and low consumption of fruits and vegetables. (All lifestyle diseases).*[5]

---

[3] Britannica.com/topic/food

[4] Science Daily. Highly processed foods dominate U.S. grocery purchases. Federation of American Societies for Experimental Biology (FASEB) March 29, 2015

[5] World Health Organization. Cardiovascular diseases: Avoiding heart attacks and strokes. September 13, 2015

- *Ultra-processed foods make up more than half of all calories consumed in the U.S. diet.* [6]
- *The US-led National Health & Nutrition Examination Survey found that 90% of the added sugar in our Western diet comes from ultra-processed foods.* [7]

If you look at the *food-like* products that fill the grocery shelves, you will see long lists of ingredients that are not food at all. They just aren't. (You can also find these convenient, unhealthy foods in about 50% of non-grocery locations such as gas stations, tire stores, vending machines in malls, auto repair shops, building supply stores, and more.) They are chemicals and highly refined and processed byproducts of a food that look nothing like its original form. We call these products, among many others, the food of The Standard American Diet (SAD). The foods that fill our SAD are more "food-like" products than real food, and are often highly refined, processed, high in fat, sugar, salt, and other chemical flavorings and additives. It is actually quite appalling what is sold as "food".

Open your cupboard or refrigerator and pull out something in a package of some sort - a box, bag, can, or wrapper, and try to read all the ingredients. To read the ingredients in a majority of our food labels (yes, a majority) just about takes a degree in scientific studies. The ingredients in the "food" are more like laboratory concoctions of fake or highly processed sugars and fats with flavorings and such. Many are preservatives, colorings, and flavor enhancers and do not represent real food. They are often addictive, fattening, and toxic to our bodies. What fills the typical grocery store shelves is "food" with too much sugar (mostly highly processed syrups), too much fat (often

---

[6] Science News. Ultra-processed foods make up more than half of all calories consumed in the U.S. diet, and contribute to nearly 90% of all added sugar intake. March 9, 2016

[7] Forbes. Nearly 60% of Calories, 90% of Added Sugars in U.S. Diet are from "Ultra-Processed' Foods. Nancy Fink Huehnergarth; March 14, 2016

the worst kinds for our bodies), too much salt, colors, and flavorings. There is also GMO foods *(A genetically modified organism (GMO) is a plant, animal, or other organism whose genetic makeup has been modified in a laboratory using genetic engineering, most common in sugar, corn, soy, wheat, canola, and animal feed.)*, along with antibiotic-rich and cruelty-full animal products. Here are a few of the chemicals you are likely to see on the labels of our most common and consumed food:

- Artificial Flavoring
- Artificial Food colorings
- Artificial Sweeteners
- Butane
- Carrageenan
- High-Fructose Corn Syrup
- Monosodium Glutamate (MSG)
- Propylene glycol
- Sodium Benzoate
- Sodium Nitrite
- Trans Fat
- Xanthan Gum

According to the Environment Defense Fund, "Thousands of chemicals were approved by the FDA decades ago, when we had far less understanding about their impacts on human health. The FDA needs to reassess their safety. Congress needs to provide the FDA with the tools so the agency can get the information it needs to set priorities and make decisions about the 10,000 chemicals in our food." [8]Unfortunately, with millions spend each year by Big Food (Big Food are the few, large companies that dominate the U.S. food market. Think Nestle, Sysco, Tyson Foods, PepsiCo, to name a few. Their products are established household names and can be found in

---

[8] Environmental Defense Fund. Reducing harmful chemicals in our food. Your family's health may be at risk, no matter where you shop.

every aisle of the supermarket.) to lobby in Congress, and with the FDA funded in large part by the companies it regulates[9], accountability for this broken system in the foreseeable future doesn't seem likely.

The warnings with these commonly used and FDA approved additives and chemicals include:

- Adverse allergic response
- Promotes hyperactivity in children
- Increased risk of thyroid tumors in animal studies
- May be linked to several types of cancer
- May cause elevated blood sugar, intestinal ulcers, and growths
- May cause inflammation, heart disease and diabetes
- May cause digestion issues such as gas and soft stools
- May be toxic to bone marrow cells
- May cause side effect like headaches
- Health issues related to this chemical include skin irritation, liver disease, and kidney problems

And this is just a list of a dozen of the 10,000 chemicals that are added into our food with a list of their known warnings. We can find these chemicals in almost every aisle in our grocery stores. You will find these additives and chemicals in boxed, bagged, canned and jar food, in the frozen and refrigerated section, down the bread aisle, the meat and dairy aisle, the baby food aisle - they literally infiltrate the food in our markets. It looks like food and does have some food in it, but it also has a long list of other ingredients that are difficult to pronounce because they are added flavorings, preservatives, additives, or colorings, and are not food.

---

[9] USA Today. Fact check: Some, but not all, of FDA's funding comes from the companies whose products in approves. August 27, 2021

When people start to understand and gain knowledge about their health and all that influences it, like the food they eat, there can be a sense of panic with that new awareness. Because these supermarket foods, along with fast and other convenient foods, have been on their table (or cars, counters, or couches) since they were little, people honestly have no idea what to eat. These foods (or food-like products) were probably symbols of their childhood and adulthood - birthdays, sports wins, family gatherings, religious holidays, entertainment, comfort food, most celebrations, and anchor and trigger them with customs, traditions, and a lot of emotion.

The truth is, the go-to foods in the Standard American Diet (SAD) are full of the stuff that is making you sick and fat: macaroni and cheese, chicken nuggets, hot dogs, yogurt, enriched cereals, chips, colored beverages and sodas, fish crackers, donuts, pastries, convenience foods, pepperoni pizza, processed meats, candy, etc. These processed and refined foods are often high in fat, salt, and sugar, which when added to the chemicals in the food products, equal a tasty, possibly addictive, food-like substance that contributes to disease and obesity.

Food has the power to heal, but the quality of food matters! A whole grain that is highly processed and stripped of its valuable nutrients in the refining process and then slathered with another highly processed sauce containing unhealthy oils, a lot of salt, food colorings and flavorings, sugar, and emulsifiers, with a side of iceberg lettuce covered in dressing that has a full day's worth of sodium in it, along with food and color additives, would not constitute a healthy or whole food meal. But that plate I just described could be considered a typical and even "healthy" plate for many.

Unfortunately, we can't trust food labeling either because they can be misleading. Many of the labels that you will see plastered all over food mean virtually nothing. That is because for most of these labels, there is no required criteria needed to put them on products. It is the food manufacturers themselves that determine if their food should have a claim on it. Therefore, although these labels may sound good or healthy, products with these labels on them do not mean that the food is healthy or good for you.

Enriched Gluten free Fiber rich/Good source of fiber Fortified Natural/Natural flavors No sugar added/Sugar free	Zero trans fat Light Low carb Low calorie Multigrain Fat free	No cholesterol/Cholesterol free No artificial ingredients A healthy choice Made with real fruit

Most of the products in the Standard American Diet (SAD) are loaded with chemicals designed to artificially enhance the flavor, look, smell, texture, or color of food. Our bodies were not designed to eat such chemically-laden food and they can cause a lot of havoc to our systems. Some known issues related to ingesting these high processed foods are: indigestion, constipation, diarrhea, leaky gut, headaches, skin issues, brain fog, food addiction, allergies, obesity, and thyroid, liver, kidney, heart, blood, and bone diseases, among other issues.

So, getting back to the question - How did you get here? It could be that your food choices line up with the Standard American Diet (SAD). It is this diet, with its excess of sugar, refined carbohydrates, saturated fat and trans fats, that is the primary cause of **obesity.** Fast and other convenience foods that have taken over our homes and kitchens leave the typical American depleted or lacking in nutrients and fiber, as they fill their plates and glasses with refined, processed, sugar-filled, and fatty foods for most, if not all, meals and snacks they consume.

A 2010 report from the National Cancer Institute on the status of the American diet found that three out of four Americans don't eat a single piece of fruit in a given day, and nearly nine out of ten don't reach the minimum recommended daily intake of vegetables. On a weekly basis, 96 percent of Americans don't reach the minimum for greens or beans (three servings a week for adults), and 99 percent don't reach the minimum for whole grains (about three to four ounces a day). "In conclusion," the researchers wrote, "nearly the entire U.S. population consumes a diet that is not on par with recommendations. These findings add another piece to the rather disturbing picture that is emerging of a nation's diet in crisis." Nutritionfacts.org[10]

Considering the addictive qualities of sugar, fats, and some of the chemical flavorings and additives in our food, it is not surprising that people find themselves in a trap of sorts, addicted to and consuming foods that continue to make them fatter and sicker.

The American author and Farmer Wendell Berry famously wrote:

"People are fed by the food industry which pays no attention to health, and are treated by the health industry, which pays no attention to food."

I believe our U.S. food system is broken and contributes to the statistics that ~70% of U.S. adults are either overweight or obese[11]. Or the statistic from the CDC that 1 in 10 adults have

---

[10] NutritionalFacts.org. Standard American Diet
[11] Healthline. Obesity Facts. Updated January 18, 2022

diabetes (over 34 million people) and 1 in 3 have prediabetes (over 88 million)[12]. This is ⅓ of U.S. adults! Another statistic from the CDC shows that heart disease is the leading cause of death in the U.S.- ~650,000/year.[13] These are stunning statistics to me and I blame our government, in large part, in association with Big Food and their strong lobby force in our government, for creating and maintaining a system that makes unhealthy, toxic, fatty food cheap, addictive, and plentiful.

The primary goal of Big Food is to make money, and they commonly place profits over the health of people and the planet. With generally bare minimum standards for sustainability and social responsibility, low quality food ingredients, and notoriously poor food governance from the FDA, it is no wonder the majority of food on our supermarket shelves coming from Big Food is subpar in nutritiousness, at best.

Then we have government farm subsidies to such crops as corn, soybeans, wheat, rice, as well as meat, egg, and dairy. The products made from these government-funded crops are found in most of our junk food in one way or another - highly processed junk food at that. The idea with these farm subsidies, also known as agricultural subsidies, which are payments or tax cuts to businesses or organizations producing food, is to make food cost less to help feed the country. This they do. However, the end result of these subsidies is often low-cost junk food and fast food. It is hard to compete with cheap food that tastes good and that has been designed with flavorings and additives to be addictive. But the results of a country eating like this are really sad, and ultimately, this is costing us on the other end, with our

---

[12] Centers for Disease Control and Prevention. National Diabetes Statistics Report. Last reviewed January 18, 2022

[13] Centers for Disease Control and Prevention. Heart Disease Facts. Last reviewed February 7, 2022

government spending in the billions every year on health care treating chronic, lifestyle illnesses.

Where do these subsidized crops end up? Well, you will find government-subsidized corn and its byproducts in thousands of products both edible and non-edible: alcohol, animal feed, baby food, bacon, baking mixes, cereal, chewing gum, condiments, hot dogs, ice cream, instant breakfast foods, jams & jellies, meat products, salad dressings, sausage, snack foods, soups, spices, and so much more. You'll find subsidized wheat also in products like biscuits, cakes, crackers, muffins, noodles, sausages, meat patties, deli meats, ice creams, puddings, cereals, and flavored rice. Subsidized soybeans are used in livestock and poultry troughs, and are processed into soybean ("vegetable") oils, and meat and dairy substitutes.

When I look at the ingredient lists of these products made from these crops, I see highly processed and highly refined foods that are loaded with sugars, fats, salt, chemical additives, and flavorings, and that are high in calories and low in nutrient-density. And THAT is what is being subsidized!

Can you imagine if the government spent a small fraction of the billions they are spending in subsidies to crops, beef, and milk, on supporting local farms that grow fresh vegetables and fruits instead? What if eating fresh, organic, local vegetables and fruits was actually cheaper than a highly processed fast-food meal? What if our food system supported healthy food choices more than unhealthy food products?

This is a big subject driven by big money that no one person will change. However, we must remember that we 'vote' with our wallet. What we buy and demand more of can create change - just like the small change you will do to move yourself in a healthier direction. We can influence this system when we know better, choose better, then put our money into supporting better, one purchase at a time.

We will talk about the power of real food to heal and restore health in Chapter 7.

Let's continue looking at how we got here in the next chapter where we will look at the dilemma of inactivity.

CHAPTER FOUR

The State of Illness with Inactivity, Bad Sleep, and Stress

Inactivity

A further reason that our health is so poor as a nation is because we are more inactive these days. Consider:

- A couple of studies published in the journal Mayo Clinic Proceedings several years ago show Americans expend several hundred fewer calories daily compared with the number they burned in the 1960's. The studies show that obese people engage in less than one minute of vigorous activity per day, and that they do only marginally more physical activity than someone who is bedridden. They also show that the typical American sits nearly the entire day.[14]
- A study from a Stanford University School of Medicine team shows that inactivity, rather than overeating, could be driving the surge in Americans' obesity. It also reported that between 1988 and 2010, the percentage of women reporting no physical activity jumped from 19 percent to 52 percent, and inactive men rose from 11 percent to 43 percent. During this same time period, obesity increased for both men and women to 35 percent.

---

[14] Yahoo! News. Vicious Cycle of Weight Gain, Inactivity Causes Obesity. By Christopher Waniek, February 27, 2014

Today, on average, one out of every three adults remains obese, which accounts for about 36% of the population. (Harvard, 2020)[15]

- According to a 2022 CDC report, only 1 in 4 US adults and 1 in 6 high school students get the recommended levels of physical activity. And, reporting America's High Levels of Inactivity, the CDC reports that all states reported more than 15% of their adults were physically inactive with individual states estimated ranges from 17.3 to 47.7% of inactive adults.[16]

- Research indicates that not getting enough physical activity contributes to heart disease, type 2 diabetes, several cancers, obesity, and can exacerbate mental illness and shorten life expectancy. In addition, inactivity costs hundreds of billions in health care costs every year.[17]

- According to studies in the UK, "The greatest risk [of an early death] was in those classed inactive, and that was consistent in normal weight, overweight and obese people," one of the researchers, Prof Ulf Ekelund told BBC News.[18]

- Other reports indicate that Inactivity is currently the world's fourth leading cause of death; 1.5 billion people around the world are so inactive they are risking their long-term physical health; and every year an estimated

---

[15] Stanford Medicine. Lack of exercise, not diet, linked to rise in obesity, Stanford research shows. By Becky Bach, July 7, 2014

[16] Centers for Disease Control and Prevention. Why Should People be Active? June 3, 2022

[17] Centers for Disease Control and Prevention. Physical Inactivity, June 7, 2022

[18] BBC. Inactivity 'kills more than obesity', by James Gallagher, January 15, 2015

5.3 million people die from causes related to inactive living.[19]

We are killing ourselves with inactivity. This is a lifestyle (habit, choice, environment) issue that we can totally change.

We sit in the car, at our desks, at our computers, at school, watching tv, on our phones, etc. We sit and sit and sit. And we get sicker and sicker. A general lack of regular exercise and our lifestyles becoming more sedentary brings us to the unhealthy state we are in as a culture and nation. As our world 'progresses' it sometimes feels like a set up for poor health. And most people wouldn't argue that over the years, with cell phones, tablets, cable TV and its thousands of channels, and our reliance on computers to function in our workspace and daily life, that we are simply sitting way more than we used to, and often with poor posture. We have created really bad habits of eating in our cars or at our desks, working long hours at a job that creates stress, watching more tv or social media, and filling up at the grocery store with a majority of processed and refined foods. Let's add in Covid-19 where so many switched to working from home and attending school from home, sitting for even more hours with Zoom and electronic overload, and binge-watching Netflix, and we saw an average weight gain of 29 pounds for those who reported undesired weight gain during this pandemic.

If you want health of any kind, you need to move. You need to stop sitting so much and move! If you are not exercising, you need to start! We'll talk more about how to start an exercise program that will lead to an exercise habit in a later chapter. In the meantime, just know that if this inactivity describes you, that you must decide to start moving if you really seek integrated health. Don't be discouraged though because there are ways to

---

[19] World Health Organization. Physical Inactivity

incorporate good, healthy movement from whatever condition or shape you are in, and even starting with 5 minutes a day will have its benefits.

Inadequate Sleep

Sleep restores and heals us, yet it is estimated that chronic sleep-related problems affect 70 million Americans of all ages,[20] that 9 million U.S. adults take prescription sleep aids,[21] and according to the CDC, 1 in 3 adults do not get enough sleep.[22] The potential problems associated with chronic sleep deprivation include heart attack, stroke, high blood pressure, diabetes, obesity, lowered immunity, depression, impairment in cognition, inflammation, and changes in appearance.[23]

With all the healing powers of sleep, why do most of us not get enough? Probably the first and most important factor is that we simply don't prioritize sleep. The tendency to put anything or anybody ahead of getting enough sleep, puts sleep towards the bottom of our priorities. Our work, social life, electronics, and screen time often take precedence over a good night's sleep. If we really knew how important sleep was for good, integrated

---

[20] Centers for Disease Control and Prevention. Sleep and Sleep Disorders. June 5, 2017

[21] TIME. Are Sleeping Pills Safe? Here's What Research Says. May 9, 2019

[22] Centers for Disease Control and Prevention. 1 in 3 Adults Don't Get Enough Sleep. February 18, 2016

[23] Cleveland Clinic. Here's What Happens When You Don't Get Enough Sleep (and How Much You Really Need a Night). March 25, 2022

health and wellbeing, we may change our priorities and commit to learning good sleep hygiene to promote good sleep habits.

Chronic Stress

Another familiar issue in our lives that is making us sick is our state of chronic stress. Stress is a feeling of physical or emotional tension in response to a challenge, demand, or fear, and like our lack of adequate sleep, Americans' health is compromised due to too much unmanaged and chronic stress. We know that stress is unavoidable in life, and occasional and situational stress is a normal and healthy response to pressures. It is the chronic, unrelenting stress that we hold in our body that takes its toll. According to the American Institute of Stress: [24]

- Americans experience more stress than the global average
- 55% of Americans report being stressed during the day
- Stress caused 57% of the U.S. respondents to feel paralyzed
- 95% of workers reported feeling stressed at work
- Today, teens have higher stress levels than in past years [25]

Of the nearly 8 in 10 Americans that report feeling stressed at least once a day in a typical week, women eclipse men in the stress match.

---

[24] American Institute of Stress. What is Stress?

[25] VeryWell Health. The 10 Biggest Teen Health Risks. By Amy Lorin. July 1, 2020

The most cited sources of stress include: work, money, the economy, family responsibility, relationships, personal health issues, job stability, housing costs, and personal safety. This kind of chronic stress leads to many unhealthy outcomes, including:

- Increased risk of heart disease
- High blood pressure, diabetes
- Depression
- Anxiety
- Accidents
- Weight gain
- Muscle tension
- Indigestion
- Irritability and anger
- Fatigue
- General dissatisfaction or worry with life.

What we know about stress is that the physiological response to stress (elevated heart rate, muscle tightening, rise in blood pressure, quickened breath, and the release of the stress hormones cortisol and adrenaline) comes from the thought of a threat, not necessarily from the reality of a threat. Our bodies *hear* our thoughts and upon hearing the threat, perceived or real, our bodies move into the stress response. This is exactly how our bodies were created to engage for protection. Unfortunately, the chronic stress that comes from perceived stress such as being under pressure, deadlines, a full schedule, regret about past or worry about the future, consciousness of lack and never enough, unresolved pain or anger, financial worries, and the general feeling of overwhelm, is doing our body harm.

CHAPTER FIVE

Limiting Beliefs and Toxic Thinking

"Every man is what he is because of the dominating thoughts which he permits to occupy his mind."
Napoleon Hill

Toxic thoughts are false beliefs that negatively influence your life and the wellbeing of your body, mind, and spirit, and can interfere with everyday functioning. These unprocessed and stuck emotions can develop from traumas, unresolved childhood issues, failure, or unfavorable circumstances, and they can turn into a chronic and toxic mindset. The habit of negative thinking is linked to increased sadness, anxiety, depression, and chronic worry. [26]The cycle of chronic negative thinking in our psyche, and their resulting toxic emotions and behaviors, create a continuous loop that feeds our sense of low self-worth and doom and gloom. This cycle is felt and experienced in our integrated being – in our bodies (illness), mind (negativity), and spirit (loss of hope).

If you are in fact, a result of the dominant thought that occupies your mind, then you need to bring awareness to your thoughts, the why behind them, and the actions that they direct.

---

[26] Cleveland Clinic. How to Turn Your Negative Thinking Around. October 3, 2019

The age-old wisdom, "As a man thinketh in his heart, so is he." (Proverbs 23:7) is the key to truly living a successful, joyful, hopeful, and contented life. This wisdom says that *you* have the power to *be* what you choose through the power of your thoughts. It really is that simple, although it may not be that easy to apply in your life. You understand and see the world not as it is, but rather as you are, and you are the product of the programming of your culture, family, society, community, and era, and what they believed, taught, and modeled. You witnessed, then came to believe and gave meaning to the concepts of love, hate, good, bad, limitations, politics, people, differences, similarities, success, beauty, honor, and just about everything you can imagine. From the food you eat, to how you keep your front yard, to the car you drive and how you smell, to the roles you play, and your inherent value as a person. These truths (as interpreted by you) were all learned and downloaded into your brain and heart as you grew up watching and listening to everyone around you. You learned and accepted what money meant, and what affection, sex, feelings, communication, work, food, spirit, home, and everything else you 'know' to be truth meant, and you did this by observing, receiving, reconciling, and then adopting these meanings as your own starting back as a very young child.

Because so many of the beliefs of *the way things are* were received and adopted so many years ago, they seem normal and there is little awareness around them. These could be considered your core beliefs, programming, or paradigm.

But these beliefs just exist in your mind, and they tell you what you believe about yourself, your values, abilities, place, role, and purpose. As a man (or woman) thinketh, so is he (or she).

So how is that working for you? Do you have beliefs that limit you living the life that you wish you could? If you want to know what you believe, look at your life. Your life tells the story of what you believe and think, more than your wishes or words do.

Look at your relationships: Do you have close and loving bonds with people whom you respect and respect you? Do you treat each other kindly and fairly? Are you able to communicate how you feel clearly to them and feel heard? Or do you find yourself in chaotic and unhealthy relationships? Do you abuse or are you an abuser - physically, emotionally, or mentally? Do you scream to get your point across? Are you easily offended, disappointed, or angry?

Look at your work. Do you get paid a good and fair wage? Are you doing something you enjoy? Do you feel appreciated and valued? Or do you feel taken advantage of, used, underpaid, or unappreciated?

Look at your finances: Do you have savings and good credit? Does spending money fill your soul? Does saving money fill your soul? Do you have too much debt or bad credit? Do you spend money on fun, recreation, vacations? Do you feel guilty on how you spend, or how you don't spend?

It can be said that the way we express ourselves and our attitudes about life are from personality traits and that may be true, especially when it comes to introverts or extroverts, and how we process and organize information in our minds. However, most of these behaviors are linked to, and led by, our deeply held beliefs, thoughts, and judgements of ourselves and the world, and they show up in the lives that we have created for ourselves. They show up in the smallest of details to the biggest matters in our lives.

Because these beliefs are embedded into our cells and go back for years and decades, changing them can be difficult. The reason for that is because we hold on to things, ideas, and beliefs that we know, and are familiar with, because change - the unknown - feels harder or scarier to us and therefore we resist it.

In The Four Agreements, Don Miguel Luiz describes the information passed down to us, and we accept, as 'agreements'. As soon as we agree to this information (that this is the way it is - life is), we believe it, and this is called faith. He goes on to say that "These beliefs are so strong, that even years later, when we are exposed to new concepts and try to make our own decisions, we find that these beliefs still control our lives."[27]

It takes awareness and intention to change a belief, especially a deep-seated belief you've had for so long. You have to identify what it is you believe in the first place, explore how you came to that (what experiences or influence led you to that belief; family, culture, past experience), reframe that limiting belief with a different, empowering belief, then work with conscious awareness to adopt that belief as your new truth or 'agreement', all while your body and mind are grooved out to do and think that known and familiar way.

I believe this is in large part the work that we do here in life - to disassemble the limiting beliefs we have unconsciously taken in or been taught, and have adopted as truth, and reassemble new, better, more abundant, powerful, unlimiting, and divine beliefs. Our beliefs, once we are made aware of them, are things that we can choose, so why not choose the

---

[27] The Four Agreements: A Practical Guide to Personal Freedom, by Don Miguel Ruiz, November 1997

most life affirming, unlimited thoughts and beliefs that you can, I say!

Please know, seeing and acknowledging your beliefs or thought patterns in yourself and others is not about putting judgment down or saying this is right and this is wrong. It is simply information that informs you about the how and why you think the way you do that drives or creates your emotions, and ultimately, the decisions and choices that you make. If your life is where you want it in the different areas of home, relationships, work, wealth, health, etc., that is excellent! Now you just may have more awareness of the *why* behind your decision-making process. If change is needed, now you know to explore your beliefs and thought patterns.

> *"A man cannot directly choose his circumstances, but he can choose his thoughts, and so indirectly, yet surely, shape his circumstances."*
> ***James Allen***

The idea is this: Your *Programming* informs *Thoughts* that lead to *Emotions* that direct your *Actions* that create your *Results*.

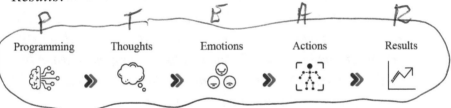

Your programming (beliefs, agreements), mostly unknown to your conscious thought, informs your thoughts (judgements, rational, perceptions) which leads your emotions (happy, sad, content, joy, fear, guilt, remorse, hate, love) which directs your actions (your behavior, choices) that determine and create your results (outcomes) in life.

Therefore, if you have an area of life that you would like to improve, identify your programming around that area, then decide and choose a more empowering belief. I will use an example from a client I worked with who desired better health but was unknowingly stuck in resentment, bitterness, and overwhelm of the many circumstances in her life. Her struggle was not food. It was her attitude and perception of being a victim and being angry at others who were creating her misery and lack of joy. It was her expectation of what her life 'should' have looked like and her deep disappointment and growing resentment that it didn't look like her expectation that created her suffering. It was her shift in thinking that changed her and improved her whole health. In her words…

"I assumed (us working together) was to plan better eating and physical activity to stabilize my weight. I had no idea and was completely ignorant of what "Holistic Health" truly meant. At first glance I was more than skeptical with my first "assignment" of completing the Integrated Life Circle, but I am so glad that I did not give into my initial response! That assessment tool, your program, and us meeting together caused an entire paradigm shift in my world. I am no longer a victim of unhappiness, unhealthy eating, and ceaseless, useless worry. Having health was about so much more than my weight, diet, physical activity, and routine medical care. Thank you for helping me learn to live everyday engaged in my life and my relationships with a renewed sense of gratitude, beauty, love, and even joy."

She made a deliberate effort to focus on changing her thought pattern from being a 'victim of this life she didn't sign up for,' to 'I have so much to be grateful for.' That shift in focus changed everything for her.

If you understand that your thinking could be the difference between a joyful life, or a poor-me existence, then the great news is that you can change it! That is the best news ever, right? No one holds the key to your life except you. You can be the champion of your life - your thoughts - your actions - your health!

If things have happened to you as a child or as an adult and you see yourself as a victim, it is time to change that perception. I know bad things happen to good people - innocent people. I also know that staying stuck with a self-perception of being a victim does not serve you or your life towards the direction of abundance and joy. You will never live your best life being a victim. You WILL have someone to blame for the reasons why you are not flourishing in your health, your job, your relationships, etc., and that blame may serve something in you, but it will never serve your higher self. No matter what has happened to you in the past, you CAN change your future and it starts with the quality of your thoughts.

As you see, our states of disease can be tied to the food we eat, our lack of movement, poor sleep quality, chronic stress, and toxic thinking. However, because we are integrated beings, we also need to think about and become aware of the other behaviors and habits that bring dysfunction, disease, or lack of health into our lives:

- Too much social media or tv
- Spending more than you have
- Lack or loss of purpose
- Lack of social connections and structure
- Alcohol or drug abuse, or any other active addiction
- Constant comparing
- Unresolved bitterness, unforgiveness, jealousy, trauma
- Lack of self-love and esteem

***

Most people are not aware of how they behave or move about in their days and lives - from what they eat, how or if they moved, or what they've been obsessively thinking about. Behaviors are so automatic (which describes a habit), that there is very little awareness of them. But, if you look at the results or the circumstances of your lives, you can see how your thoughts, and therefore the resulting, mostly unconscious behaviors, express themselves loud and clear. It is sometimes only in the awakening of where you don't want to be (sick, medicated, depressed, obese, alone, angry, etc.) that you awaken to the desire or need to change. Maybe that is why you are reading this book - because you are ready to make a change that will move you into better health, more joy or presence, or better relationships. No matter where you are right now, you've come to the right place.

It is time to take control of your life. No one is going to do that for you. In the next chapter, I will give you an assessment tool called the Integrated Life Circle to help you identify your current state of integrated health. Once you complete this, you will be able to see at-a-glance where your health could use fortification, or where it is already strong. This is where we START with ONE!

CHAPTER SIX

Your Integration Identified

*"A healthy person has a thousand wishes,
but a sick person has only one."*
Indian Proverb

Now that you have an understanding of some of the factors that may be creating imbalance or poor health in your life, it is time for you to do some self-assessment. In order to help quickly assess your integrated health, I have created the *Integrated Life Circle*, designating 3 areas of living to help you identify where you are feeling satisfaction and balance, or dissatisfaction and imbalance. Although we don't segment our lives into neat and distinct sections, for assessment purposes, this tool will help you see the different regions of your life in their perspective area. The areas of the *Circle* include:

BODY: Nutrition, Exercise, Sleep, Stress Management, Physical Health, Physical Environment

- This is your physical health - how you feel in your body. Consider: the health of your bones, muscles, organs, and tissues, your immune system and your ability to heal; the quality of the food you eat and the balance of your nutrients; your body weight and Body Mass Index, aka, BMI; your lifestyle habits (smoking, taking drugs, prescription medications, consumption of alcohol, sleep habits, tension you carry, how you manage stress, exercise or movement habits); your energy level, and your environment as it relates to clean air, water, work and home environment, and safety.

MIND: Self Esteem, Finances, Education, Work/Career, Quality of Thoughts, Emotional Environment

- This is your mental and emotional health. Consider: how you feel and talk to and about yourself and others; your relationship with money and spending or saving; your satisfaction with your level of education, work, and career; your general thoughts about life - positive, negative, optimistic, pessimistic, paranoid, content, eager to live, excited for adventure, fearful, feeling that life is hard/unfair/grand; your perceived levels of stress or tension; and your environment that supports negativity or positivity.

SPIRIT: Joy, Life Purpose, Play, Relationships, Spirit/Faith/Belief, Creativity, Gratitude

- This is your spiritual or soulful health. Consider: your sense of purpose and excitement or dread for life; your level of trust, peace, and joy, or fear, distrust and unease or angst; your ability to enjoy the life you have as you are right now; your healthy and loving or your unhealthy relationships; your faith and belief in a greater good/cause/spirit and how that influences your life; the connection to your own personal creative power in your gifts; and your level and attitude of gratitude that you live with.

With this tool, you can discover and identify which areas of your life need more energy, support, and time spent on them to bring balance and harmony. Each area plays a part in your overall feeling and healthy beingness.

This will be something you look back on as you are traveling in your journey of improving your integrated health, and it will show you, even when you don't feel it, just how far you've come, committing to one consistent action at a time and growing from there.

Integrated Life Circle

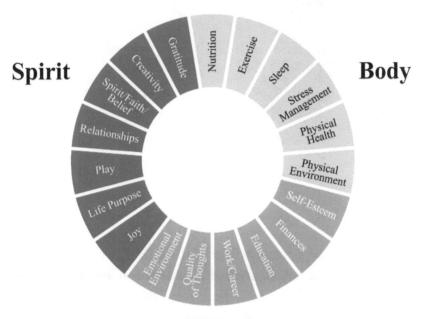

Completing your Integrated Life Circle:

1. Place a dot in each category to indicate your level of satisfaction or dissatisfaction within each area – the closer to the center of the circle indicates dissatisfaction - the periphery indicates satisfaction. Connect the dots to see your Integrated Life Circle.

2. Identify imbalances, then determine what areas of your life you can spend more time and energy on to create balance.

Integrated Life Circle

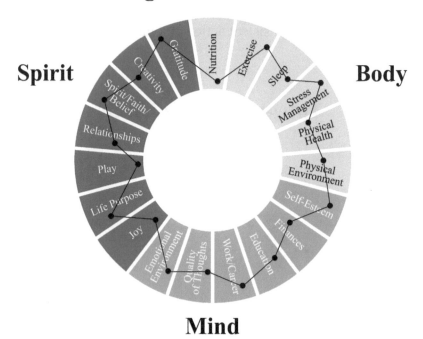

Spirit

Body

Mind

This example of a completed Integrated Life Circle could indicate support would be helpful in the areas of Nutrition, Joy, Health, Play, and Finances. It would also indicate satisfaction in the areas of Self-Esteem, Stress Management, Life Purpose, and Work/Career.

The following chapters will look at different areas in the *Integration Life Circle* and how they connect in your integration of mind, body, and spirit. Once you have identified your Circle, you will look at outlining behaviors that you can practice so you understand how you can START with ONE healthy decision, and one healthy behavior, to nourish your body, mind and spirit to create positive change in your life. In time, with awareness, commitment, a plan, and consistent, small behaviors, you will be rewarded with better health.

Part III

THE POWER TO INTEGRATE & HEAL

CHAPTER SEVEN

Food to Heal

*Food isn't like medicine, it **is** medicine.*

Let's start with understanding the power food has to heal us. The seven main classes, or elements, of nutrients that your body needs are proteins, carbohydrates, and fats (also referred to as macronutrients), vitamins, minerals, fiber, and water. Where do we find the best and most nutritionally dense elements? The best food for life (health, disease prevention, weight management, energy, creating, birthing, being) is REAL, WHOLE FOOD.

Whole food is grown or raised: fruits, vegetables, beans, whole grains, nuts, seeds, dairy, eggs, meat, fish and poultry. It is food that is as close to its natural or original state as possible, nutritious, unprocessed (or minimally processed), and free of chemical additives.

It is important to understand that the food we eat is information our body uses to create new cells, feed the good or bad bacteria in our gut microbiome, create the building blocks for the blood, tissues and hormones that instruct our body and brain to move and breathe, decide the level of energy and stamina we have, and many more functions. The better quality information, the better quality cells and outcomes.

The 3 macronutrients in our foods are Protein, Carbohydrates and Fats and each are vital for a balanced and well-functioning body and brain.

- Protein supports cell growth and repairs damaged cells. In this process, proteins produce new tissues for growth and repair, and support the maintenance and regulation of body functions.
- Carbohydrates supply your primary energy source of glucose as your body breaks down your food into this simple form. Fiber is also a vital part of the carbohydrate macronutrient and helps your digestion and your waste system work. Carbohydrates also supply many of the vitamins, minerals and phytochemicals (active compounds found in plants) that support healthy bodily function and energy.
- Fat supports absorption of fat-soluble vitamins, such as A, D, E, and K, helps to insulate your body to keep you warm, helps to make essential fatty acids from your food which supports healthy cell membranes, hormone production, healthy development and functioning of the brain, nervous system, skin, hair, immune and inflammation responses, blood clotting, among many other processes.

How food affects the health of our minds and guts.

The food you eat is the building blocks to the hormones that regulate so many of your bodily functions - from your metabolism, sleep, emotions and mood, energy, and your sexual function. The quality of your hormones, in large part, relate to the quality of food you eat, not only as building blocks, but also the environment that is created in your gut, where many hormones are made.

This is where food and mood are connected. The science of the gut-brain connection is discovering the integral connectedness that what you eat affects the condition of the gut and therefore impacts not only our physiology, but also our psychiatric conditions and disorders. In an April 2020 National Library of Medicine article, it states,

- "Previous studies have shown that a majority of the gut hormones mainly play roles in the central regulation of appetite and food intake; however, recent studies suggest that they are also closely related to other physiological processes, for example, inflammation, that can be linked to different brain disorders, such as anxiety and depression." "It is now well accepted that a majority of the gut hormones play an important role in the regulation of food intake in the CNS (central nervous system). Most intriguing, obesity and mood disorders often tend to co-exist. There are several gut hormones... that are identified with known roles in mood disorders, such as anxiety and depression."[28]

If someone wants or needs to know, there are nutritional recommendations for ADD, depression, anxiety, Parkinson's, MS, mental illness, allergies, brain fog, addiction, and just about every 'issue' one may experience. Many of them focus on eliminating or reducing animal products, processed foods, and sugars, while adding whole-food plants such as fruits, vegetables, beans and legumes, whole grains, nuts, and seeds. There may be specific recommendations for particular issues, but most of the recommendations refer back to whole, minimally processed foods with a large variety of plant foods.

---

[28] National Library of Medicine. Gut Hormones in Microbiota-Gut-Brain Cross-talk. April 2020

An example of healing through diet is from a friend of mine, who was diagnosed with a rare auto-immune disease. Her condition progressed and as it did, it became more and more debilitating, at times leaving her unable to walk. She was told that the only treatment options for her were immune-suppressing drugs and blood transfusions a few times a year. When she asked her doctor, who was a specialist in this auto-immune disease, if she needed to adjust, eliminate, or add anything to her diet, he told her that her diet had nothing to do with her condition.

Intuitively, she knew this couldn't be true and dove into her own research. Her findings led her to a healing protocol of only whole foods, including a variety of vegetables, organic animal meat, and whole grains. As she followed this protocol, her body began to heal. Her symptoms were virtually gone.

After having regained her health and experiencing little to no symptoms, a cross-country drive had her stopping at a truck stop to eat unhealthy and highly processed foods. Within hours, her ability to walk was impaired, as if her body was in full rebellion again. This proved to her that her health would only be maintained with clean, whole foods. This experience led her to become a nutritional therapist and she now helps others treat themselves with food and nutrition.

The point here is that no matter one's issue - obesity, heart disease, depression or other mood-disorders, autoimmune disease, mental illness, or neuro-diseases such as Parkinson's and MS - eating nutritional, clean, whole, unprocessed foods can help the body feel better, reduce or slow progression of illness or disease, or reverse them all together.

In the previous chapter, I mentioned that how we got so sick as a nation is in large part due to our broken food system. It's a fact that much of the food here in America is processed. From our nation subsidizing an abundance of GMO'd corn, wheat, soy, beef and more, to seemingly nothing off limit as far as chemicals being allowed into our food system. And from our habits of eating out and too much fast food, to the Big Pharm and traditional medicine in our "health care" system offering band aids (medications) for the consequences of poor diets and lack of movement, we end up with poor health.

But there IS good news! There is a movement, an openness to awareness and learning that is happening! The Food-as-Medicine movement is growing and becoming more known to the general population, if not in depth and in practice, at least as a concept. Functional and holistic medicine is also more well-known and there is an understanding by many that going to the doctor and leaving with another medication is not the golden answer to our health problems. Farmer's markets are popping up in cities and small towns and more and more people are looking for locally grown, in-season, and organic food there.

I love the 400BC wisdom from the "Father of Medicine", Hippocrates, when he said,

"Let thy food be thy medicine and medicine be thy food."

This ancient and wise knowing is as relevant as ever today in our toxic food system. But what does this mean?

It means, the better quality food we eat from plants and animals, the better the body can do all of its natural functions, like grow, think, move, breath, detoxify, heal, feel, and restore, to name just a few. The food we eat informs and dictates the quality of processes, functions, and new cell growth that our body is busy with every second of every day. In this way, food is not *like* medicine, it *is* medicine. So, what does this *medicine* look like?

Well, what is the ingredient in asparagus, or an apple, or whole oats? How about whole grain brown rice, lentils, spinach, an egg, black beans, walnuts, or blueberries. How many ingredients are in an almond, quinoa, or grass-fed, organic beef, roasted vegetables, corn on the cob, a fresh peach, plum, or an orange?

These real, whole, unprocessed foods don't need a list of additives, flavoring, colorings, emulsifiers, acid regulators, preservatives, etc. because they are simply nature's food from the earth. That is our medicine!

In a Yale University analysis on the health benefits of a balanced diet of fruits, vegetables, grains and legumes, they found that "a diet of minimally processed foods close to nature, predominantly plants, is decisively associated with health promotion and disease prevention."[29] Is this something that you've never heard before? I doubt it. We all know that eating more whole foods is better for our health, right? We may not abide in that knowing, but we know it on some level.

The bounty and gift of plants

"I give you every seed-bearing plant on the face of the whole earth and every tree that has fruit with seed in it. They will be yours for food."
Genesis 1:29

With many issues arising from eating animals (antibiotic & steroid use, GMO feed, inhumane living conditions, stripping land for animal lots, large amounts of resources - food, water, land - needed in proportion of food benefit) and with more science understanding and acknowledging the life-giving benefits of plants, the trend is the promotion of a primarily plant based diet. And there is a good reason to love plants.

---

[29] The Atlantic. Science Compared Every Diet, and The Winner is Real Food. 2014

Plants provide fiber and nutrients like no other, namely, phytochemicals ("Phyto" refers to the Greek word for plant). The variety of more than 25,000 natural chemicals called phytonutrients can be found in plant foods and the best way to be assured to get the beneficial elements is to eat them in their natural form: fruits, vegetables, beans, legumes, nuts, seeds, whole grains, teas, herbs, etc. Plants also contain all of the elements of nutrients in them (proteins, carbohydrates, fats, vitamins, minerals, fiber, and water). Studies show the natural compounds found in plants support healthy bodies and immune systems, help prevent disease and aid in keeping your body working properly. Their supportive role in our health is vast and include many health benefits:

- Supports and boosts immune function
- Reduces risk of disease (heart disease, diabetes, cancers)
- Reduces inflammation which reduces the disease and pain processes
- Increases antioxidant activity
- Supports healthy digestion
- Heals the gut

If eating animal protein and products are important to you and you feel they help you feel better balanced, dietetically and physically speaking, then my recommendation is to eat as clean and humane of animal products as possible. Here are some labels to look for when buying animal products and what they mean.

Look for these labels and certifications when purchasing animal products – from meat to cheese to dairy.

USDA Certified Organic

When applied to beef, the U.S. Department of Agriculture (USDA) Certified Organic means the beef product have met the following requirements:[30]

- Fed 100% organic and GMO-free feed and forage (but is not required to be grass fed).
- Raised in living conditions accommodating their natural behaviors (i.e., the ability to access and graze on pasture).
- Never administered antibiotics or hormones.

When applied to poultry, USDA Certified Organic means the poultry product have met the following requirements:[31]

- The birds must be raised organically no later than two days after they hatch;
- They must be fed certified organic feed for their entire lives. Organic feed cannot contain animal by-products, antibiotics or genetically engineered grains and cannot be grown using persistent pesticides or chemical fertilizers.
- It is prohibited to give drugs, antibiotics and hormones to organic birds (please note: federal regulations prohibit the use of hormones in raising poultry).
- All birds must have outdoor access.

Grass Fed

Grass and forage shall be the feed source consumed for the lifetime of the animal, with the exception of milk consumed prior to weaning. However, grass fed cows may still receive

---

[30] U.S. Dept of Agriculture. Organic 101: What the USDA Organic Label Means. March 13, 2019

[31] U.S. Dept of Agriculture. Supporting Organic Integrity with Clear Livestock and Poultry Standards. Feb 21, 1017

supplemental grain feed or be "finished" on a fully grain-based diet.

Grass finished

Cattle received a grass or forage diet their entire lives - no grain fed finish.

Pasture raised

A "pasture raised" claim on meat, poultry, dairy, or egg labels means that the animals were raised for at least some portion of their lives on pasture or with access to a pasture, not continually confined indoors. On beef or dairy, it does not mean that the cows derived all their nutrition from grazing on pasture or that they were 100 percent grass fed. There are no common standards that producers must meet to make a "pasture raised" claim on a food label, no definition for "pasture," and no requirement for the claim to be verified through on-farm inspections.

Humane Farm Animal Care (HFAC) Certified Humane® "Pasture Raised" space requirement is 1000 birds per 2.5 acres (108 sq. ft. per bird) and the fields must be rotated.[32]

Free Range

The USDA has defined the term "free range" only for chickens, not for eggs or for other livestock, such as cattle. According to the USDA, chickens must be "allowed access to the outside" to be considered free range. This does not necessarily mean they roam free outdoors, returning to their coop only during inclement weather or at night. It can also mean they spend all their time in

---

[32] Certified Humane. "Free Range" and "Pasture Raised" officially defined by HFAC for Certified Humane Label. January 16, 2014

cramped, indoor pens that have a small open access to the outside. There are no USDA rules for eggs or other animals when it comes to free-range labeled products. In this way, it is up to the producer themselves to decide what that means when they label their products free range.

HFAC's Certified Humane®, a private certifying organization, certifies poultry "Free Range" and requires a space requirement of 2 sq. ft. per bird. The hens also must be outdoors, weather permitting, and when they are outdoors, they must be outdoors for at least 6 hours per day.[33]

Cage-Free

On an egg carton, "cage free" means that the hens that laid the eggs were not raised nor confined in cages. It does not mean that the hens had access to the outdoors, and it is likely they were stocked at high density with little space to live.

A "cage free" claim on chicken adds no value as meat chickens are not raised in cages, but in large, open structures known as "grow out houses" (enclosed barns). Meat chicken houses typically house tens of thousands of birds and grant less than a square foot of space per bird.[34]

GMO Free / Non-GMO

GMO stands for "genetically modified organism." The definition of what it means to be genetically modified is hotly debated still, but when you see something labeled as non-GMO, it usually

---

[33] Certified Humane. "Free Range" and "Pasture Raised" officially defined by HFAC for Certified Humane Label. January 16, 2014

[34] The Humane League. What Do "Cage-Free" Eggs Labels Really Mean? Mar 17, 2021

means that the genetic makeup of the plants and animals used in the product has not been altered for the purposes of food[35]

Humanely raised

There is no legal definition for the term "humanely raised." The USDA's Food Safety and Inspection Service (FSIS) does not explain what "humanely raised" means. There are a few organizations that privately certify animal welfare standards, such as HFAC - Certified Humane®, Animal Welfare Approved, Global Animal Partnership (Whole Foods), and American Humane Certified. They all have different animal welfare standards and requirements for their members in their programs for chickens, beef cattle and pigs.[36]

Sometimes all these labels actually can lead to more confusion. It is probably best to stick with an organic label then pick from what other concerns you have regarding animal welfare and get to know what that means specific to the product that you want to consume. It is also possible in many parts of the country to visit small, local farms that grow and raise food, if you want to see for yourself. Goodmeatbreakdown.org states they are a collective of farmers, ranchers, butchers, land-owners, educators, business owners, and nonprofit leaders that considers land, animals, and people. They may be a good resource to learn more about producers, farmers, butchers, label information, guides to meat, and other reading and informational resources about the industry.

What people eat can be medicine or poison. With all the fast and convenient foods, our home cooking has declined, and we only know how to heat things up. Junk In, Junk Out. With Big Food dominating the space at our supermarkets and on our streets, we

---

[35] Non-GMO Project. What is a GMO?

[36] Environment Working Group. Decoding Meat and Dairy Product Labels

need a new cultural paradigm shift to real, whole foods, and a return to home cooking as a way to heal our bodies. When we bring in real, whole, unprocessed (or minimally processed) foods, we simply work better – body, mind, and spirit. Learning what to eat for better health and how to cook and prepare healthy food can transform people's lives.

A wonderful example of food as medicine is the program called "Shop with your Doc" offered by Hoag Health in Southern California where they send doctors to the grocery store to meet with any patients who sign up for the service, plus any other shoppers who happen by with questions about nutrition or good food choices. This program is an effort to make food a formal part of treatment, and to try to prevent, limit or even reverse disease.

Or, the Therapeutic Food Pantry program at Zuckerberg San Francisco General hospital that offers patients several bags of food prescribed for their condition along with training on how to cook it.

Another beautiful example of this awareness of food as medicine is the Certified Culinary Medicine Specialist program that provides clinicians with nutritional knowledge and culinary skills so that they can effectively incorporate healthy eating into patients' diets and deliver optimal patient care. Their classes include: The pediatric diet, Cancer, Celiac Disease, Neurocognition, IBS/IBD /GERD, Polycystic ovary condition, and more.

Loma Linda University School of Medicine offers specialized training for its resident physicians in Lifestyle Medicine that is a subspecialty in using food to treat disease.

There are nutritional counselors, coaches, and therapists who work with individuals wanting to improve their health or reverse disease through food nutrition and lifestyle changes.

The truth is, *you* can begin to change your health today and bring the Food as Medicine Movement into your life by making even small, consistent changes to what you are eating. For example, if you replaced ONE fast food or other convenience food a day with a plate of real, whole foods - mostly plant-based - your body would respond almost immediately. You could literally feel better after one meal - less bloating and inflammation, less lethargy after eating, an easier bowel movement, less brain fog, etc. If you honor your body by feeding it clean, wholesome food, it will honor you right back! Now if you did this consistently, it is very possible you could see results with weight loss, better blood sugar levels, clearer thinking, and lots more. If you changed one meal, then another, then another until you were eating a majority of clean, whole foods, you would be a new person!

Consider the benefits of eating whole foods:

- Your body will detox (from toxins, excessive fats, sugars, salts, chemicals)
- Food cravings will reduce
- Hunger will be stabilized
- You'll experience better mental clarity and focus, less brain fog, improved ability to concentrate
- You'll be able to eat plenty without weight gain
- Better energy, more stamina
- Weight loss
- Improved sleep
- Less bloating and discomfort and more regularity
- Improved skin

- Reduction of pre-existing health conditions: headaches, joint pain, IBS, constipation
- Improved performance – energy, exercise, overall movement
- Improved blood levels – blood sugar, cholesterol levels, blood pressure
- Improved bone health
- More confidence and happy as you feel, think, and look healthier

People will say to me, "Okay, I get it - eat more veggies. But I don't know how or what to buy, how to cook or prepare healthier foods, and I don't even know if I like the taste of them." Fair enough. We don't know what we don't know and what we weren't taught, or have not practiced. I don't care how old you are - many of us grew up with fast, unhealthy, processed food and that is what we know.

First of all, even if you know you need to totally revamp your way of eating, need to heal from a lifestyle disease, or have guilt for how you have nourished yourself or your family, just take a deep breath and trust that your body will thank you for each and every small bits of goodness that you offer it. Your body will respond with kindness back to you as you begin nourishing it with real food in the right quantities.

One sure and easy way to begin eating better is to add vegetables and greens to ONE meal a day. Most people simply are not eating enough fruits and vegetables. You can begin to change this and START with ONE added leafy greens or other vegetable, or a fruit to what you are already eating. One way I do that is I add greens (leafy greens: spinach, lettuces, arugula, bok choy, kale, collard greens) to whatever I am eating, be it eggs, lentils, rice, toast, sandwich, beans, etc. I either use my greens as a base to put my other food on, or I add the greens over my food. I can add other vegetables as well: tomatoes, sprouts, squashes, corn, celery, fresh herbs, etc.. If I am having oatmeal or yogurt, I will instead add my fruits, berries, walnuts, pumpkin or chia seeds, to get in my added plant power. If you bring awareness to the intention of adding in your healthy fruits and vegetables to one meal a day, your new behavior will be much easier to adopt for a second or third meal, or an eating out meal, or even a snack. Think about what food you already eat and then brainstorm about how you can add some healthy vegetables, fruit, or healthy plant power to it. This is how the START with ONE thing works – we keep adopting one change and soon, we are progressing with another one thing, then another, and so on. With those changes added in, you can more easily crowd out unwanted behavior, and as you do this, you will find better health and feeling better will follow not far behind.

Here are a few apps that help identify healthier food options:

EWG Healthy Living App - Scores Food and Personal Care Products Skin Deep

Foodvisor app - Identifies Food and gives breakdown of calories and macronutrients

OpenFoodFacts app – Food Quality Scores

RecipeIQ app - Recipe organizer and Nutrition Calculator

SIFT app – Food Label Scanner

Yuka app – Food & Cosmetic Scanner

There are so many resources out there to help simplify food preparation, and for easy-to-make recipes with just a few ingredients. There are also many online guides and tons of recipes for a slow cooker or Crock Pot, and a pressure cooker or Instant Pot.

There are thousands of cookbooks to fit your fancy, but here are a couple of my favorite cookbooks. I like them because they emphasize using whole, in-season foods to nourish the body, mind, and spirit.

America's Test Kitchen: The Complete Plant Based Cookbook

Eat Complete: The 21 Nutrients That Fuel Brainpower, Boost Weight Loss, and Transform Your Health - Drew Ramsey M.D.

EATING WHOLE: Easy & Healthy Whole Food Plant Based Recipes - Michele Swaczyna

Fast Food Good Food: More than 150 Quick and Easy Ways to put Healthy, Delicious Food on your Table - Dr. Andrew Weil

Love Real Food: More Than 100 Feel-Good Vegetarian - Favorites to Delight the Senses and Nourish the Body: A Cookbook - Kathryne Taylor

The Plantpower Way: Whole Food Plant-Based Recipes and Guidance for The Whole Family: A Cookbook - Julie Piatt and Rich Roll

The Whole Truth - The Eating and Recipe Guide - Andrea Beaman

True Food: Seasonal, Sustainable, Simple, Pure - Dr. Andrew Weil

And here's a few fun and inspiring Instagram accounts to follow for recipe inspiration, plant-based cooking, and nutrition resources:

@just.ingredients

@themodernnonna

@veganrecipesideas

@healthygirlkitchen

@meatlessmonday

CHAPTER EIGHT

Movement, Sleep, and Stress Management to Heal

The food that we eat affects our health in a huge way, but equally important is our daily movement and exercise. Moving improves everything!

Studies have found that "people who completed 30 to 40 minutes of moderate to vigorous activity had a substantially lower risk of early death—similar to those who had very low amounts of sedentary time."[37] In other words, if you have a job or reason that you sit for many hours a day, you can still offset the hazards of sitting for a long time with daily exercise. Movement is our fountain of youth, but most people don't move enough these days for the development of strength, agility, stamina, and energy.

There cannot be enough said about the power and importance of movement. We are designed to move – to walk, change physical planes (standing, sitting, pivoting, turning, lunging, etc.), to push, pull, and lift. Movement keeps our joints lubricated and injury free, our tendons healthy, our skeletal and muscular systems moving well and without restriction. Movement also causes muscle tissue to produce proteins that have important disease-prevention and anti-inflammation functions.

---

[37] Men's Health. You Need 30 to 40 Minutes of Daily Exercise to Undo the Damage of Sitting All Day, Research Says. By Selene Yeager, January 21, 2022

CDC's Exercise Recommendations:[38]

- *Adults need to do two types of physical activity each week to improve their health–aerobic activity and muscle strengthening:*
- *150 minutes of moderate-intensity aerobic activity per week or,*
- *75 minutes of vigorous-intensity aerobic activity per week, plus at least 2 days a week of muscle strengthening activity. Anything that gets your heart beating faster and/or makes your muscles work harder than usual counts.*
- *Is it moderate or vigorous? Use the "talk test" to find out. When you're being active, just try talking:*
- *If you're breathing hard but can still have a conversation easily, it's moderate-intensity activity*
- *If you can only say a few words before you must take a breath, it's vigorous-intensity activity.*

There is deliberate exercise, such as jogging, walking for exercise, weight lifting, HIIT (high-intensity interval training), martial arts, swimming, gymnastics, cycling, wrestling, and tennis, that is done intentionally and that builds stamina, strength, agility, and cardiovascular health.

Then there is N.E.A.T. movement – Non-exercise activity thermogenesis. This is the movement that we find we do throughout the day that is non-exercise related: walking up and down the stairs, in the store, or at our job. It is when we are cooking, playing, cleaning, gardening, working, and even standing. It's also sometimes called non-exercise physical activity, or NEPA.

---

[38] Centers for Disease Control and Prevention. How Much Physical Activity do Adults Need? June 2, 2022

All movement matters.

Although we do have guidelines and recommendations about how much exercise to aim for every day and week, we also know that ANY exercise is good! Studies show that even short bursts of physical activity – mini-workouts – can be just as effective as one concentrated session. Even brief trips up and down stairs count towards accumulated exercise minutes and reduced health risks, says a Duke University School of Medicine study. But the intensity has to reach moderate or vigorous levels.

Benefits of Exercise on the Body:

If you want to feel better, have more energy and add years to your life, exercise. No matter your age, gender, or physical ability, everyone benefits from exercise.

- Exercise boosts energy and stamina. When you exercise and work your cardiovascular system, oxygen and nutrients are delivered to your tissues, supporting heart and lung health resulting in more energy, endurance, and muscular strength.
- Exercise helps control weight, prevent disease, and supports a good immune system. Regular exercise helps weight management by supporting weight loss and excessive weight gain. It also helps manage or prevent many health problems, including: Type 2 diabetes, stroke, metabolic syndrome, many types of cancers, arthritis, high blood pressure, cardiovascular disease, bone health, and more.
- Exercise promotes better sleep. Regular exercise can help you fall asleep faster, get better sleep, and deepen your sleep.
- Exercise improves your sex life. Feel-good hormones released during exercise raises mood and self-esteem, or

body image. Regular exercise also enhances sexual performance - think better blood flow, strength, flexibility, stamina, and less stress.

Benefits of Exercise on Your Mood, Aging & Quality of Life:

- Exercise improves mood. Movement, especially vigorous exercise, is a great stress reliever, but even a brisk walk can help. Physical exercise releases brain chemicals that support a happier and more relaxed mood and helps relieve anxiety and tension.
- Exercise can bring fun into your life. For all the reasons listed above, regular exercise leaves us feeling better – healthier, sexier, less stressed, more attractive, calmer, and more energetic. Take all of this and add fun! Connecting with others to move in a dance class, hike, pickleball, tennis game, racquetball, basketball, group exercise class, rowing team, track or running group. All these activities can bring healthy friendships and support to live your best life and have fun doing it!

Benefits of Exercise on Your Brain:

- In addition to all that, our brains LOVE exercise! It's like a supercharge for the brain!
- Exercise produces new brain cells helping improve attention, memory, focus, and reaction times.
- When you workout consistently, the more your hippocampus and prefrontal cortex grows and becomes 'stronger'. This helps to stave off neurodegenerative diseases and aging disease, like Alzheimer's and will protect your brain from incurable diseases

The goal or idea with movement is not to pursue burning calories or even fitness, per se. It's about integrating movement back into our days so that our bodies function well and comfortably for the life that we want to live.

Consistency is key.

Having a consistent practice of something you love to do lets you reclaim movement as a part of your integrated way of being, versus just being something that you must do or achieve. There is no shortage of resources to support and encourage movement these days. There are:

- Exercise apps
- Virtual trainers and classes
- Youtube videos for just about every activity
- Gyms
- Parks
- Bike and walking paths
- Studios offering cycle classes, dance, yoga, Pilates, stretching, strength classes
- Senior centers
- Public tennis and Pickleball courts
- Public or private pools
- Online support and accountability groups

One small thing that I have adopted into my day is 1:00 minute of counter push-ups while I think about and say aloud things that I am grateful for. I just lean my body over my kitchen counter or desk or even kitchen table for one minute and connect with gratitude while I get some daily exercise in! This has been one very small thing that I have added that supports my physical body and my spiritual and emotional body. And the gratitude helps me to think better when I need a reset.

I love the story of Bobby J. who was in the weight management program where I work and whose couch-to-marathon story is so inspiring. He joined the weight loss program at 303 pounds in the summer of 2019 at the age of 34 with blood pressure in the Stage I Hypertension range. Five months later, he weighed in at 216, having lost 87 pounds, with his blood pressure now in the Ideal range. It was around that time that he started to move his walking into running and in October of 2019 ran his first 30 minutes without stopping. He remembers it being grueling, but felt quite accomplished when it was done. He continued to run and reminded himself that a 6 minute mile and a 15 minute mile is still a mile and although he wanted to become a faster runner, that he was nevertheless becoming a runner, even if he was a slow one. Within months of his first non-stop 30 minute run, he began training for a half marathon set for the Spring of 2020. Even though that race was canceled, due to Covid 19, as was the half marathon race he signed up for that summer, and the California International Marathon scheduled for the winter of 2020, Bobby kept running.

In February 2021 he joined a men's workout group where he found the camaraderie and community he needed to diversify his exercise and encourage his running. Finally, in December 2021, Bobby ran his first official race - the California International Marathon, and he finished it! It wasn't easy - he had pain, cramping, and major fatigue along the way to the finish line, but he crossed it! His greatest lesson? That he feels like he can do anything! Bobby's decision to seek help to help him lose weight, inspired his journey from the couch, to walking, to running, to finishing his first marathon!

He started with one goal (to walk) and once he accomplished that one goal, he upped it and committed to another one, and so on and so on. It wasn't always easy, but it was worth it! Today he continues his runs and workouts with his buddies, and has incorporated and maintains healthier habits in his everyday life using the skills he has learned and his own set of personal rules around his behavior, which are the strategies he feels works best for him. Some examples of personal rules might be not to eat after 7:00pm or to do at least 10 minutes of strength work each day.

If you are not currently getting consistent movement and exercise in your days, it is time for you to START with ONE! Exercise is too important to miss for so many reasons and you just simply will feel so much better when you move! And…. sleep well!

"Let her sleep, for when she wakes,
she will move mountains."
Napoleon Bonaparte

Ahhh…. A good night's sleep! There is nothing like it. Sleep heals and restores us - body, mind, and spirit. When our bodies are at sleep, they are healing machines, working to repair tissue, bone, and muscle, from our heart to our blood, and to our brains, sleep restores us! Some of the benefits of good sleep:

Improves:
- Memory
- Physical appearance
- Mood
- Ability to focus
- Decision making
- Alertness and creativity
- Ability to lose weight
- Immune function

Helps reduce the risk of:
- Cancer
- Depression
- Inflammation
- Stress

Getting good quality sleep is fundamental and significant to our health. Learning and adopting good sleep habits to improve your sleep health is worth all the effort. Here are some things to consider when creating better sleep hygiene:

- Keep a consistent sleep schedule - go to bed at the same time each night and get up at the same time each morning
- Create a relaxing bedtime routine - take a bath, turn off electronics at a certain time, dim the lights, read a relaxing book, sip some calming herbal tea, meditate, gentle stretching
- Get some exercise during the day, and limit your caffeine and alcohol before bedtime

If you are one of the many that do not get adequate sleep (~7-8 hours/night), deciding to make sleep a priority can be a game changer for you and your health. One definite way to help you get better sleep is learning how to reduce your stress response.

"It's not the load that breaks you down, it's the way you carry it".
Lou Holtz

As mentioned, living in a state of chronic stress is unhealthy and damaging to your wellbeing. But the good news is, you can learn to reduce and manage your stress and change the state of your body, regardless of what is going on around you. One significant way is by slowing down and taking deep breaths. Scientific studies show that the simple act of controlling your breath can help manage stress and promote relaxation.[39] Shallow or hyperventilation that can accompany a stress or panic state, can actually prolong and worsen the feelings of anxiety. Controlling your breath with slowed down nose breathing can improve some of these symptoms. A relaxed breathing pattern calms the

---

[39] National Library of Medicine. How Breath-Control Can Change your Life: A Systematic Review of Psych-Physiological Correlates of Slow Breathing. Sep 7, 2018

nervous system and brings the body into a more relaxed state, and supports physiological changes that include:

- lowered blood pressure and heart rate
- reduced levels of stress hormones in the blood
- improved immune system functioning
- increased physical energy
- increased feelings of calm and wellbeing.

There are many breathing approaches and techniques to calm your body. Practicing just one of these techniques for even one minute can make a shift in your physical state. Here are just a few that have shown to reduce stress and anxiety:

Belly Breathing - Place one hand on your upper chest and the other hand on your belly, below the ribcage. Breathe in slowly through your nose and exhale slowly through slightly pursed lips.

4-7-8 Breathing - Place and keep the tip of your tongue against the ridge of tissue behind your upper front teeth for the duration of the exercise. Close your mouth and inhale quietly through your nose to a mental count of four. Hold your breath for a count of seven. Exhale completely through your mouth, making a whoosh sound to a count of eight. (Start with only 4 cycles and move up to max of 8 cycles with practice.)

Alternative-Nostril Breathing - Alternate-nostril breathing involves blocking off one nostril at a time as you breathe through the other, alternating between nostrils in a regular pattern.

Box Breathing - Exhale to a count of four - hold your lungs empty for a 4-count. Inhale to a count of 4 - hold the air in your lungs for a count of 4.

Resonance Breathing - Gently breathe in through your nose, mouth closed, for a count of six seconds and exhale for six seconds, allowing your breath to leave your body slowly and gently without forcing it.

Start practicing a deep breathing technique one to five minutes a day and you will notice a difference in your state of being. When you start to feel your body move into a stress or anxiety state, use one of these breathing techniques to calm your body. You always have this tool (your breath) wherever you go! Learning to manage stress will have you feeling and thinking better, and experiencing more joy.

In addition to the above-described breathing techniques, try any of the following suggestions to relieve stress:

- Regular exercise
- Healthy social connections
- Getting adequate sleep
- Laughing more
- Journaling
- Yoga, tai chi, or qigong
- Prayer, Meditation, or guided imagery
- Bonding with your pet
- Practicing being in the present moment
- Change the way you look at what's troubling you

Add in an awareness of gratitude or love with your breathing or other activity, and you'll really experience a reset!

CHAPTER NINE

Thoughts to Heal

"A man's mind may be likened to a garden, which may be intelligently cultivated or allowed to run wild; but whether cultivated or neglected, it must, and will, bring forth. If no useful seeds are put into it, then an abundance of useless weed-seeds will fall therein and will continue to produce their kind."
James Allen

Thoughts are things. They are the seeds of things to be. If you want health, abundance, joy, great relationships, you must take responsibility for your thinking, your emotions, and your actions, and create what you want. Staying stuck in reasons why you can't do this or that, or how life is unfair, or how you are just an unlucky person, or your self-limiting thoughts, serves no one. But what it does do is keep you where you are. That may be unhealthy, unhappy, negative, victim-focused, depressed, or sick.

Changing your thoughts has the power to transform your life. The first step in change is awareness. Remember it is your thoughts (from our programming) that feed your emotional state, that then have you act or behave in a certain way, that create the results in your life. Bringing awareness to what thoughts you dwell in much of the time gives you the option to choose what thoughts you want to feed, or starve. What you focus on, grows. In this way, if you focus on positive and abundant thoughts, you will create positive and abundance outcomes in your life.

You can go all the way back to your programming to identify what and why you believe what you believe. You can explore family beliefs, traditions, and the culture you grew up in to discover some of your thought origins. This can be intense work as you awaken and begin to question everything about what you believe to be right and true. You can see some of these beliefs in the smallest of things or the most profound things you hold dear. I remember when I used to see a tattoo, it meant that either the person was a biker dude or was in the service overseas. This is because when I was growing up, we just didn't see many people with tattoos and the ones we did see were kind of scary (they must be in a dangerous biker gang or soldiers). My dad had a big tattoo on his arm from his Marine days and in my young mind, I attached that to mean a connection with a drunken fighter, as that was what my dad was at the time. I remember seeing more and more people with tattoos over the years and when I first saw them, my paradigm (beliefs about these people) was really challenged. Then as I saw more and more women getting them, and men who obviously weren't in a bike gang or a former soldier, I started to loosen my grasp on that belief. I thought, Why is 'everyone' getting tattoos? It just took a while for me to reconcile a new way of thinking about tattoos. I find myself more curious about them now, which shows me that the judgment that I had around my thoughts about tattoos and the people that had them have changed.

The idea is that one can't be curious and at the same time judgmental. Curiosity to me is a good sign. I ask people about the stories behind their tattoos now. Some are very special, marking a dear memory. Others are silly, representing a night of folly and drunkenness. Either way, I recognize my programming has changed, and for that, I am thankful.

This may seem like a small and even ridiculous program, paradigm, or belief, especially to younger people who grew up with a very different perspective about tattoos. I could agree now, but to me, because of the era I was raised with the cultural norms and passed down perspectives, this was a normal and accepted perception. Tattoos were taboo. Go ask someone you know who was born in the 50's or 60's about what they remember about the attitudes or perceptions around tattoos when they were growing up. Heck, it was only in 2021 that Disneyland announced that it was going to allow employees to show their tattoos while on the job!

We all hold on to silly and limited thinking about the things we see and come across every day. Whether seemingly small and silly, or serious and profound, we hold beliefs and therefore, perspectives about everything. Unless we are consciously curious, we may stay unaware of most of these beliefs.

What do you think about when you see or hear...?

- Nude sunbathers
- Someone skydiving
- Domestic abuse
- A woman wearing a hijab
- An introverted studious type of person
- Violence on tv
- Marijuana
- Same sex people kissing
- Bikers riding through your town
- Street people living on the sidewalk
- Someone smoking or drinking alcohol
- An obese person eating at a restaurant or sitting on a plane
- Wearing shoes in the house
- People dancing to their own beat
- Old people
- People eating rodents or insects
- A stay-home dad
- A strong executive woman
- Hard Rock or Rap music, or a church choir

These are everyday things that we all have a thought about - a conditioned thought, based on some belief we have about them. But these things are normal and acceptable in some cultures and unacceptable in other cultures and societies. How about the judgment on people who cuss, are handicapped, gay, a different color or religion, eat certain foods. How about guns, war, masculinity and femininity, drugs, gangs, or murder? What do you think when you see a person with mental illness walking down the street talking or shouting with no one near them?

What meaning do you give these? What feelings come up for you based on the meaning (thoughts/beliefs) you give these? Fear? Judgment of right or wrong? Righteousness and superiority that you do or don't do this or that, and they should or shouldn't? Are you grossed out? Do you find it normal and fun? Does it make you feel free and happy? Whatever it prompts in you, it is based on a belief you have about what is good or bad, right or wrong. What if it's neither?! What if it is just different? No one can answer this except you, but it may be worth going back to the where and how you received these cultural opinions as truth in the first place. William Shakespeare conveyed in one of his plays, the Hamlet, that "There is nothing good or bad, only thinking makes it so". Does this thought alone prompt a strong reaction in you? To bring awareness or to become aware of your beliefs, you must be willing to identify what and where you are in your thinking of something, and then be open to being curious. Remember, one cannot be both truly curious and judgmental at the same time.

Another example of a small thing given distorted meaning is this story: a friend told me he recently uncovered in therapy that he was holding onto resentment towards his dad for a look that he perceived to be unapproving and unloving when he was 12 years old. He held onto this grief for 50 years based on his 12 year old perception of a look! His 12 year old self gave meaning to a look his dad gave him, and he internalized it as bad. He felt unaccepted, then got angry. That unexpressed anger turned to resentment that he kept deep inside of him for years. Although it became an unconscious resentment, it showed up in his attitude for all those years, and it blocked a free and loving relationship with his father.

The thing about our thinking of others and things in a certain way is that when we do this, we can't help but put these limitations, or judgements on our own self. We should or shouldn't do this or that. We can or can't do this or that because of this or that - it's not right, acceptable, possible, probable. What do you tell yourself that you can or cannot do every day? What you say after the words, "I am", or even the verbs you choose after the word, "I", can be very telling about your personal beliefs or your own sense of self-worth and value.

Your inner dialogue is written all over your life with:

I can't ....workout, run, travel, find my soulmate, leave my job, buy a house, write that book, speak in front of others, lose weight, say my truth, forgive that person, stick with anything, go after my dreams, do this or that...because..... (a limiting belief or paradigm); **I am** ...too fat, old, dumb, embarrassed, ugly, lazy, mean, inexperienced, tired, uptight, fearful.... ; **I hate** ... exercise, cooking, my work, my home, my life, my body, the way I look, this world....; **I could never** do that -- It's too big and **I am** too small. Those kinds of dreams are for other people who are smarter, better, richer, or prettier.

OR

I can... accomplish, achieve, create, love, give, work, manifest, find, call, forgive...; **I am**... love, light, kind, joyful, grateful, intelligent, willing, capable, eager, excited, happy, forgiving, thankful.... **I can do and create** what I want in my life because I am the master of my thoughts and I understand that my thoughts ultimately feed my actions, which gives me results.

All that you tell yourself is a story, and the choice and power to think anything you want and create a new story is yours. Just know that what dominates your thoughts, comes to be.

"We mentally conceive the form and then think life into it."
Thomas Troward

The power comes when we become aware that *thoughts are things*, or at least the seeds of things to be. When we believe in what we think about with a strength of conviction and emotion, whether it be the emotions of fear, doubt, joy or gratitude, the things that we think about breathe life into them. The life and energy in our thoughts, and then our emotions, lives in us. We attract reciprocal emotions and energy, and the results are manifested in action, behavior, mood, and in material expression. The growth of our thoughts from an unseen idea in our mind to its manifestation in the physical world, depends on how you nurture them - feed, water, or starve. Your mindset, which is the direction of your thoughts and state of belief, is crucial to any change.

I remember when my husband and I started talking about building a house. We would explore ideas together while talking about how many bedrooms we needed, what we wanted the space to feel like, the lighting and view, etc. We then hired an architect and started sharing our thoughts with him about what we had in our minds. Soon enough, he designed some house plans based on our ideas and we had our thoughts on paper, literally. We hired a contractor and someone to help design the interiors, and two and a half years after our first thoughts of building our home, we moved in. Our ideas gained energy as we got excited about creating our home. This energy fueled our action and connections to other people who helped us build our home. But it all started with an initial spark of a thought.

Here is another example of a not so unusual battle and how thoughts can create results: You are 75 pounds overweight and getting sick and tired of being sick and tired. You say that you want to lose weight. You decide that you are going to start to exercise, eat less, and consume healthy food. You start out strong with daily 15 minute walks and you clear your pantry out of its junk and fill it with healthy and nutrition options. You are happy because after the first week of being consistent, you lose 3 pounds and already feel a difference. Woohoo. You are doing great.

The next couple of months are going well and you remain consistent with your walks and healthy food choices. You are down 20 pounds now and feeling proud of yourself. You get a call that your Aunt Tia passed and that you need to go to Florida to help your family with the service and support. Your emotions are high, and sadness fills you. Your way to deal with loss was always with food. What do you do now? *Well, just a little won't hurt. If you just eat a couple of servings of this, you'll be fine and return to your healthier way when you get home.*

Being with your family especially during this sad and difficult time triggers so many emotions in you that you indulge in your proven friend to help soothe you - food. *Ahhh, there it is.* It helps for the moment. But then you start to shame yourself telling yourself, *DANG! I've blown it. Look at me! Just say no, won't you! Damn it! Okay..... I'll get back to it when I get home. I'm just going to let go while I'm here.* You continue to revert to familiar ways to deal with family, pain, stress, and find yourself 10 pounds back up when you get home a week later. *What the heck is wrong with me? It's so hard to get back to healthy eating and movement now that I've been away for a little more than a week. Okay.... I'll start back tomorrow.* But those familiar, shaming voices start telling you that you didn't really have a chance to lose that weight. That you will always be fat so just accept it. You know how to live as a fat person, plus, food is your friend.

Before you know it, you have regained all your weight back plus some. Now you feel super bad about yourself, reinforcing in your mind and spirit that you are a loser who can't even complete or follow through with a diet that will get you healthy. *I guess I don't deserve to be healthy.*

Oh, the torture of the mind and our thoughts! This is just an old story that you believe about yourself. Changing your story, especially if you've had it for years and possibly decades, takes awareness and a new, replacement story. Changing your story and perspective is 100% possible!

Take the sad news about Aunt Tia and change it to relationship troubles, a heavy workload, a stressful environment, a change in life or lifestyle (a move, a child born or graduating, a new job....), a remembrance of trauma. Life and all its offerings, "good" or "bad," can be triggers that can have us running in the direction of the known way, and that known way starts with our thoughts. Our body, mind, and spirit find comfort in the known, even if it's destructive.

This is the work of change - any change. It will always start in our mind and with our thoughts. Bringing awareness to our thoughts and the stories that are keeping us stuck, is the first seed of change.

"You never change things by fighting the existing reality. To change something, build a new model that makes the existing model obsolete."
R. Buckminster Fuller

The way to do this is to think about what you WANT, not what you don't want. Don't fight the old behavior that you don't want, build the new! What do you want? What does it look like, feel like, smell like? What do you want to create for yourself? Good physical health? - what does that look like? Less or no medication? Strong muscles? The ability to garden or play with your kids? The ability to ski, or hike, or climb like you used to? Does it mean feeling better in clothes and feeling sexy in your body? Is it a healthy marriage, job that you love, a sense of love and appreciation for yourself, or the freedom from guilt, bitterness, or blame? Whatever it is, picture it! Create the picture and feel the emotion of it (love, joy, freedom, pride, abundance, hope, gratitude, connection, openness). Then focus on THAT! Let that be your fuel, your picture, your why, your inspiration. Do not think or dwell in where you are now.

However, you can still experience a loving self-acceptance of your state at this moment. Rejecting your current state is not the goal. It's bringing in a NEW and healthier vision into your being. Fill your mind with the picture of health, love, and abundance that you want to create. Commit to that picture throughout your day, everyday, and let it help you make decisions as it runs through the process of thoughts - emotions - actions. Keep the focus on the picture of what you want to create then embrace it. Feel the feeling of joy when you buy that beautiful new dress and wear it for the first time. Revel in the pleasure of laughing with your kids as you all are playing on the playground. Experience the pride of receiving that promotion and pay reward; or the exhilaration of skiing down your favorite mountain with perfect snow! Make your self-talk match your accomplished desire. When you change your story in your mind, you change your life!

The story of Roger Bannister who broke the 'unbreakable' 4-minute mile in 1954 shows the power of having a vivid vision. Throughout recorded history, until this day in May of 1954, runners from all over the globe tried and failed to break the 4-minute mile barrier. It was thought impossible to run this fast. But Roger believed the impossible was possible. He was known to close his eyes and visualize his run, step by step. He would see the image of himself crossing the finish line and could hear the crowd cheering – all in his mind – and he created that vision in the physical world being the first person to run a sub four-minute mile. The runners of the past had been held back by a mindset barrier that believed running a sub four-minute mile was not possible. When the mindset barrier was broken by Roger (known as the "Bannister Effect"), others saw that they could do something they had previously thought impossible. Within the same season, another runner ran a sub four-minute mile, and within two years, there were 10 sub four-minute runners on the books. Today there is an elite group of around 1,660 sub four-minute mile runners. How Bannister achieved the 'impossible' was through mindset and he inspired others of what was possible. We all have a four-minute mile barrier in our life. It's possible that what you consider impossible just may not be.

In a principle called the Power of Assumption by Neville Goddard[40], he teaches that to change anything in your life, you have to change the beliefs and assumptions you hold about it. This is exactly what Roger Bannister did!

Just like Roger, keep the vision of what you want, add in the emotion of how it feels to BE IN that place right now, then live in that space. This vision is the seedling of realities that fuels your actions and outcomes accordingly. Use new words to describe yourself as you experience the emotions of being and creating the life that you want. Remember, whatever you say after "I am..." has energy and power to move you in a direction! I am love, capable, energized, joyful, grateful, unstoppable, enough,

---

[40] The Law of Assumption. Neville Goddard

beautiful, talented, gifted, in service, excited that I am creating the life that I want!

Then ask yourself: What and how does someone who is … (healthy, successful, creating their dream, happily married, confident, loves life..) do and act? Then DO that! When I got the leading to write this book, I didn't have any experience with writing like this. But believing that I was assigned to write this, I thought to myself, what does an author do? Well, they write. They write something towards their book a little every day, or most days. They schedule time to write and contemplate and dream about their vision for their writing. So that's what I did. I thought like an author. I scheduled time to sit down most days to write. I carried around a notebook for thoughts that came to me throughout my day. I envisioned this book as complete, helping people get healthier. I envisioned YOU being inspired to START with ONE thing that moved you in a healthier direction even before one page of this book was written!

Support your affirming and high-vibe thoughts with reading books that support this idea and acknowledge the power of your thoughts. Extend yourself to be around people who think big, have faith and believe that all things are possible. Nurture healthy relationships and serve others in areas that you feel so on-purpose with. Watch or listen to podcasts, music, tv, or documentaries that are uplifting and crowd out the violent tv shows, negative news, naysayers, or victim stories, with what you WANT to create.

"Finally, brothers and sisters, whatever is true, whatever is noble, whatever is right, whatever is pure, whatever is lovely, whatever is admirable—if anything is excellent or praiseworthy—think about such things."
Philippians 4:8

The instructions for us to think upon such things are not just words. This is divine wisdom that will lead us to a fulfilled life. This is how we transform our mind - by thinking such things. Think of it like this - 95% of success is in your mindset, and 5% is in your plans. Not only are we called to think higher thoughts for true integrated health and wellness, but we also must call on the emotional superpower that connects us with Power, and that is gratitude.

Science says that when you bring your attention to the things you are grateful for in your life, your brain works better. Research has found that **people who practice gratitude on a regular basis are healthier,** have a greater sense of well-being, an increased ability to navigate difficult circumstances, and experience stronger relationships. [41]

So what does gratitude look like and how can we get better at it? **Gratitude is a state of being** - a way of looking at your life and finding things to be grateful for. It looks like making a conscious decision to feel satisfied with what you have instead of focusing or longing on what you do not have. Practicing gratitude is just that - a practice. It is something you get better at the more you practice. A gratitude practice has you looking at your world through a lens of thanksgiving and seeing that each moment of your day presents you with an opportunity to be appreciative for something. Finding even the smallest of things to be grateful for in challenging times keeps open glimmers of hope and faith that it's going to be okay. And if you are practiced at finding and expressing gratitude, you may even find the challenging time or circumstance itself is something to be grateful for - as an opportunity to grow, feel, mourn, gather, and heal.

There are many ways to practice gratitude:

---

[41] Harvard Health Publishing. Giving Thanks Can Make you Happier. August 14, 2021

- **Be mindful of what you are thinking or saying**. Look for things in your life to be thankful for and express gratitude and appreciation for people, places, things and circumstances.
- **Pray gratitude prayers.** Many spiritual traditions include prayers of gratitude. Say prayers of thanksgiving for all you have and all that you can give away - from your home and belongings, to your work, friendships, and especially, love.
- **Be generous.** Giving connects you to your own sense of gratitude and thanksgiving. Give of your time, talents, and resources, and do it on a regular basis.
- **Write down things that you are grateful for.** Start a journal and consistently write down the things that you are grateful for during your days. It is good to do this throughout your day or before you go to bed. Make a list. You find what you are looking for. So then, if you set out in the morning looking for things to be grateful for throughout our day, you will find them. Knowing you will make your list at the end of the day makes your day expectant with eyes and open hearts to find goodness.

However you practice gratitude, bring it into your everyday life. Soon, it will be a more automatic thought and you will find gratitude filling you up and leading you to a more joyful life!

CHAPTER TEN

Self-Love, Grace, and Forgiveness to Heal

"How you love yourself is how you teach others to love you".
Rupi Kaur

Self-love has been defined as having a high regard for your own well-being and happiness and taking care of your own needs. It is about loving yourself well, with respect, kindness, acceptance, grace, and boundaries. When you have these kindnesses for yourself, you can have them for others. You've probably heard the saying "Be the change you want to see in the world," which embodies the wisdom of self-love. If you practice self-love and experience this kind of compassionate acceptance towards yourself, and extend it to others, you make the world better. When you love and respect who you are, you are more free and better able to love and respect others.

Self-love can look like:

- Not looking for your worth in other people
- Not measuring your worth in your productivity
- Not measuring your value by how your body looks
- Speaking to yourself with kind compassion
- Not taking what others say or do personally
- Being patient and gracious with yourself, especially when you make a mistake or are learning something new
- Accepting what you cannot change

- Saying no without hesitation or explanation
- Not worrying about others' opinions
- Letting go of toxic people in your life
- Putting your phone down
- Knowing and accepting yourself
- Not comparing yourself to others
- Standing up for yourself
- Practicing healthy boundaries
- Taking good care of your body
- Doing things that bring you joy
- Forgiving yourself and others
- Trusting yourself and your intuition
- Seeing yourself as a gifted, created being and developing your talents
- Finding, following, and serving in your gifts and passions
- Surrounding yourself with positive people
- Giving yourself a pep talk
- Being impeccable with your word (mean what you say and say what you mean)

This sounds lovely, yes? Would you describe yourself as loving yourself? Do you ever put yourself down or compare yourself with others? Do you make excuses or limit yourself about why you can't do something? Do you make up reasons or agree with people on the reasons why they treat you badly?

> *"The most important conversations you'll ever have are the ones you'll have with yourself."*
> *David Goggins*

We are all works-in-progress. All of us. The voice inside your head has most likely been a long time in the making, probably since your childhood. Maybe your parents, schoolteacher, aunt or uncle, next door neighbor, babysitter, sibling, frenemy (friend + enemy), boss, or stranger spoke a word, phrase, or criticism of you and fed a wound inside you. Maybe you are jaded or hurt from a wounded person who didn't love themselves, or who simply didn't know better. Words or acts, intended or not intended to hurt, may have confirmed in your psyche a 'truth' that you were not good enough as you are. These 'truths' about yourself (as you believe them) make the idea of complete self-acceptance of who you are, not seem right or possible. Or having loving compassion towards yourself feels like a big lie and something that you are not worthy of.

The truth is – you are worthy! You possess and are made with the Spirit that made all of creation. You are a spirit with a body. You were created to be connected to the infinite – God, or your Higher Power - and have been given unique gifts, talents, passions, and purpose. You are a miracle!

If you take this in and believe it, truly believe it in your heart, mind, and bones, then you must see yourself differently. You must see yourself with the grace and love that you are made from.

"For you can render God and humanity no greater service than to make the most of yourself."
Wallace Wattles

This topic of self-love may not seem relative to changing a habit to eat more vegetables, get more sleep, or start a walking routine, but it is intimately connected. When you love yourself, you don't harm yourself. You take better care of yourself. That is not to say that bad habits instantaneously go away, although they can. But a behavior or habit that is not a loving act towards yourself, stops jiving with how you want to treat yourself.

The abusive self-talk, the screaming fights, the over indulgence, the spending your rent money on alcohol, drugs, makeup, or shopping, hanging around people who put you down (and vice versa), the constant expectation on others and the followed disappointment, hanging on to the job that sucks the life out of you, always settling for less, seeing yourself as a powerless victim – these behaviors are not the expression of true love, whether it be to yourself or others.

What you think about yourself, shows up in your life. If you want your life to be different, you can begin with the thoughts and beliefs about yourself. START with ONE loving or empowering thought or message directed to yourself. Or START with ONE kind act towards yourself. If you don't know where to start, look at the list in the first part of this chapter and pick ONE of those actions to begin.

Whatever ONE thing you start with, be consistent and practice it or say it throughout your day, every day. Remind yourself that you are a gifted and talented person with a birth-given mission. Tell yourself that you are worthy of love and respect. Respect yourself by only affirming positive and affectionate thoughts about yourself. If you find yourself comparing yourself to another, or putting yourself down, quickly reaffirm that you are a spirit of love who is growing and learning and becoming.

Grace

That we are (again) all works-in-progress, allows for constant grace. Awww, grace – *courteous goodwill; do honor or credit to (someone or something) by one's presence, the free and unmerited favor of God, a divinely given talent or blessing.* [42]

Grace rocks!

Grace is like an umbrella - it covers you and protects you from the elements - the elements of your critical self, others' opinions, your fears and insecurities, and your previous failed attempts at

---

[42] Oxford Languages Dictionary

getting healthy. It changes your 'failures' to lessons and these lessons will be used to grow compassion and wisdom. This growth can be used in service to yourself and others. There is no room for beating yourself or others up when grace covers you.

Grace speaks of kindness, a gift, space to be, forgiveness, and acceptance of self and others. To me, grace covers our transgressions and errors, and our failed attempts. Yes, there are consequences to behaviors that are unhealthy or unwise. But even living with the consequences of our choices, we can still experience grace.

What if you loved yourself exactly as you are, this very minute, as-is right now? The beautiful experience of grace is acceptance without conditions. Loving yourself well inspires you to take better care of yourself - to rise up and be the person you are called in your soul to be. Love and acceptance exactly as you are. All you need, you already have inside, and it's released and inspired to act when led with grace. This is often the catalyst to change. We let go of the critical self - the self-judging self - and accept. This acceptance, with grace, is what motivates desire and actions to change. It gives you hope as well, with love and compassion, to be better – to love yourself better.

I talk to so many people who shame themselves everyday about their failures to get healthy, lose weight, continue to smoke/vape, not exercise, eat poorly, not forgive, keep the job, or stay with the abusive person, and basically keep doing the things they don't want to do. They often shrug it off or pretend it's not a big deal, only to later cry and feel full of shame, humiliated or embarrassed. It's understandable to feel all these things. But the truth is, the shame or guilt felt doesn't help the situation one bit.

This is where grace comes in - loving favor. Okay, maybe you messed up again and didn't honor your word to yourself, but every moment of every day you have a chance and a choice to choose differently. Beating yourself up, criticizing your poor decisions, or telling yourself how much you stink are not helpful! In fact, when you are doing this - putting yourself down and reminding yourself how much of a failure you are - you are talking to your unconscious mind and to every cell in your body, reinforcing those negative thoughts, emotions, and messages on a physical and energetic level. What is real or what is imagined, whether it be pain from the past or worry about the future, impacts your body and brain, which affects your wellbeing.

> *"You are allowed to be both a masterpiece*
> *and a work in progress."*
> *Sophia Bush*

Know this: you are worthy to live a life of love that is full of grace, and this life starts with you. You determine what you will believe about yourself and therefore your value, and what you deserve in this world. With awareness and intention, you can become the person you want to become. With mindfulness, you can choose better quality thoughts – thoughts that empower you, that create possibility, abundance, and a lot of love in your life. These thoughts will feed your emotions that drive your actions. The actions will bear evidence in your life. And your thoughts about your failings or fallings can become thoughts of victories when you see them as gifts to learn and become better.

In what area of your life can you give yourself grace? Where can you be more kind, loving, forgiving and patient with yourself? Identify an area in your life that you can give yourself the acceptance of being both a masterpiece, and a work-in-progress. Then, START with ONE gracious act to practice every day that brings that grace to life.

Forgiveness

Forgiveness is vital in our journey of better integrated health. As I said earlier, our cells hear our thoughts, and they respond negatively to the stress of unforgiveness, and conversely, positively to the reconciliation that forgiveness brings.

Forgiveness and letting go of bitterness can make way for improved health and peace of mind. Forgiveness can lead to:

- Healthier relationships
- Improved mental health
- Less anxiety, stress and hostility
- Lower blood pressure
- Fewer symptoms of depression
- A stronger immune system
- Improved heart health
- Improved self-esteem
- Lower risk of heart attack
- Improved cholesterol levels
- Improved sleep
- Reduced pain

The opposite is true as well. Being bound by unforgiveness and grudges can:

- Bring anger and bitterness into every relationship and new experience
- Prevent you from enjoying the present
- Bring on depression or anxiousness
- Prevent connection to meaning or purpose in your life
- Put you at odds with your spiritual beliefs
- Lose valuable and enriching connectedness with others

"Resentment is like drinking poison and waiting for the other person to die."

I have personally experienced the power of forgiveness in my life, and it was so profound, I believe it changed the trajectory of my life. I grew up in a large and wonderful family, but we were achingly impacted by an alcoholic and violent father. The fear and scars of bitterness that planted in my soul during my childhood started to ripen and begged to be released in my 20's. At the time, I didn't know what was going on with me, I just knew I was ripe in emotion, crying at the simplest question of, Are you okay? In my wisdom, I sought counseling, where I learned about the turmoil of my insides, the fear and anger I was storing, and I revisited my 5-year-old perspective of a drunk and angry father. Resentment and bitterness were pouring out of me, and I wanted to be clean from the swirling negative feelings and anger that I had built up towards my dad.

With direction and support from my counselor, I knew that I needed to forgive my dad and that the time was now. With God's mercy and grace, my dad had by then been sober for many years, yet my child's eyes and heart could only see and receive him with the fear of the child I was when I was so hurt and afraid of him. My perception and belief of who he was, a monster, had not changed even though he had. I was stuck and I was ready to be freed.

The circumstances that brought this moment to be was nothing short of God's perfect and divine timing. To say that all the stars aligned would not be overstating it. On the same day that I committed to talk to my dad face to face, was the same day that he had said he was going to come over to help me with something, something he had never done before. Here we sit - me scared, raw, and ready, and I literally poured my heart, hurt, pain, and anger, out to him. I told him I wanted him to tell me how sorry he was for the torment, and fear, and violence he did to our family. I cried from the deepest part of my belly. I cried while gasping for air, almost convulsively crying. He sat, cried, and listened. He apologized. No excuses. He shared some perspective of his awful brokenness during that time in the height of his alcoholism.

I forgave him completely. My inner child was free. I felt it. I still do. I remember the next day I literally could see differently - the trees, nature, me - everything looked different. It was like I took off some dingy glasses and now I could see. I saw him differently as well. I saw his tenderness toward people, his redemptive life of serving the community of those afflicted with addiction. I saw a man who suffered greatly, and in his own way, still did, from the pains he caused people. I saw a man that I loved and admired and was so proud of. That moment changed me. It was like a before and after of me. And the funny thing is, I didn't even know that I was stuck before that. I appeared to have it all together, but deep down in the innermost part of me - my child - was still scared and angry, until I wasn't.

We all can experience freedom from bitterness, anger, and resentment through forgiveness. Sometimes it comes in incremental releases, other times, like mine with my dad, it comes in a complete washing.

There are so many reasons to let go of unforgiveness - body, mind, and spirit. But how do you begin the process of releasing bound up bitterness, anger, and resentment towards a person or people who have hurt you? You START with ONE simple, doable action. Here are some examples of one thing you can start with to begin your journey of forgiveness:

- Say a daily prayer for yourself and the offender

- Admit and recognize the value of forgiveness in the quality of your life
- Move away from seeing yourself and identifying with your role as a victim.
- Join a small group or seek individual counseling that can help you process your emotions and help prepare you to forgive
- Read books, or listen to sermons or speakers on the subject of forgiveness
- Connect with a safe and wise person in your circle to share what you are going through

The decision to let go of the past and forgive yourself or others is an act of love, most especially to yourself. Forgiveness can be a process so be patient with yourself and give yourself grace as you heal and journey through the process. Understand that the freedom and reconciliation in your heart and mind that you receive from forgiving others does not necessarily mean reconciliation with the offender. Be willing to let go without any expectation of another person.

I remember teaching a class on Aging Well to a middle-aged group of men and women where I shared about food, movement, social connections, and emotional health, including forgiveness – of self and others. When the class was over, I asked the participants what subject they connected to the most. Most of them shared they related to being stuck in anger, bitterness or unforgiveness. I remember feeling a bit surprised that of all the things shared that day, it was unforgiveness that seemed to trap them. And at the same time, I wasn't surprised. Forgiveness is a deliberate and gracious act for oneself and others, and pride, ego, and self-righteousness must be moved over to experience the full fruits of deep forgiveness. It can feel very vulnerable, scary, and unfair to walk through the process of forgiveness, but if you do it, your body, mind, and spirit will thank you.

Part IV

START WITH ONE

CHAPTER ELEVEN

Your Why

Probably the most important steps in thought and behavior change is your *why*. This is the **reason** you want change in your life. This is the fuel and inspiration of a better future. Your reason, or why, to make a change may be a new awareness or purpose that was sparked inside of you. Your why may have been prompted by fear of all that you are losing or will lose if you don't change. Or it could be fueled by the hope of feeling stronger and healthier. When you follow your why, you will most likely find more purpose and joy. It could look like:

I want to.... be able to live out my purpose here; see my kids or grandkids grow up; show up as a better parent, partner, member of my community; be remembered for something good; get off these damn medications; be able to play, ski, garden, travel, walk, fly, love, and live with the freedom of a body that moves better; develop and serve with my gifts and talents; live boldly; feel more alive.

Your why may have been sitting in your soul for years calling out to you. Now I am calling you out. If you are reading this book, you are ready to ACT. No more waiting. No more reading books on how to change, or getting more information so you can start, or waiting for the perfect time when all the stars and planets align, and you feel ready. More knowledge does not create change – ACTION does.

Just trust the calling and the reason you picked up this book. You are ready. You don't need anything more to begin. Whatever is calling you to become, bring it to life in your mind. Bring it to a clear, wonderful, emotional vision in your mind. Whatever you want to create in your life will always first start in your mind. Every experience in the physical world is the result of an idea or dream in the unseen world. We talked about this in the chapter Thoughts to Heal. For this purpose, use your imagination and picture yourself having achieved your why. Create that clear mental picture, then allow yourself to feel the joy, happiness, contentment, freedom, accomplishment, pride, and empowerment that reaching that goal feels like, then feel it now. Experience it as if you are already there.

This vision and these emotions are the seed that you will water and feed. Not unlike planting a peach tree today and picturing yourself picking those yummy peaches that your tree will produce in its future. In this example you can see yourself joyfully picking a beautiful peach and taking a bite of that juicy fruit with a smile on your face. You planted that seed and you cared for the tree, and now you are receiving the fruits of your seed.

Your why is just like the peach seed. Plant it today, and picture it with joy, in its fulfillment. Don't wait to feel the joy of the peach until it's in your hand. Experience the wish fulfilled now, and care for your vision with daily 'food' of emotion, belief, and faith.

I so appreciate this example of one of my group participant's why for getting healthy and losing weight. The first thing he knew was **what he wanted** - to proudly walk his daughter down the aisle in his nice tailor-made tuxedo. His **why was love** for his daughter and making this moment special for both of them. When he joined the group, he had to lose significant weight to get to his vision. With intention and determination, he has kept his vision (both of what he wanted and his why) alive in his mind – feeling love, pride and dapper - and it consistently has motivated him to make better choices, even when it was hard. His daughter's wedding is in a month, and he will most definitely be wearing his tux!

Know within. The importance of your imagination to create a new vision of your why is vital. This vision is the seed of your becoming. Without the new seed, nothing new will grow. It is important that you keep this vision active in your thoughts and mind, for the process of belief to take root, just like my participant did for his daughter's wedding. You do not need to know or try to figure out exactly how you will create this vision into being right now. Just create it with vision, focus on it with your thoughts, and then feel the emotions you will feel when it comes to be in front of you. Soon you will believe it, your subconscious will receive it, and its physical creation will be put into motion. The fuel of your why, and your becoming that person in your vision, will create new thoughts and motivate new behaviors in you. It will begin an exchange of energy that will bring things and people into your path that you could not see before.

> *"The outer conditions of a person's life will always be found*
> *to be harmoniously related to his inner state."*
> *James Allen*

How do you keep this vision active and really start believing on a deeper level that you are in fact becoming and creating your why right now? Repetition is how. All the beliefs and visions you have about yourself and your life reside in your subconscious and conscious minds. They got placed there through years of repetition. Your new vision will find its way into your thoughts and beliefs the exact same way. If consciously fed and nurtured, your new belief (vision, paradigm, concept) will crowd-out outdated and unproductive visions through repetition.

You can START with ONE vision of your why by writing it down in detail. Envision it and then write down what it looks like, smells like, feels like. Who and what are you doing? Picture it and note even the smallest detail. This is the building of the new model of what you want to create and the emotional connection to the reason why you want to create it.

If my why was to create a healed relationship, my vision may look something like:

I see me and this person crying together with joy and deep bonding as we share and listen to each other. They heard me, and I them, and we have a new understanding and compassion for what took place. I feel clean with forgiveness and so much love and gratitude for them. We are laughing together like we used to, and I feel like this is the best medicine for my soul.

If my why was to create money in the bank, my vision may look something like:

I open my bank statement and smile with pride at how much I have saved over the past year. I am excited at all the possibility this money is providing me. Opportunity is knocking and I am ready now that I have this money in the bank. I am confident in my ability to create my life the way I want it and dream big.

If my why was to create a strong, fit body, my vision may look something like:

I feel so good in my body and I am able to move and play as I have always wished. I am so happy that I am skiing again, and I feel so strong on the mountain. I feel the fresh, cold air as I ski down, and I am full of gratitude that my body is perfectly fit for this activity that I love. I am proud of all the work that I have done so consistently to build my body strong.

Consider the visions of a why for:

- A found soulmate
- A thriving business
- Health and happiness
- Fulfillment of a dream
- Traveling the world

Remember, your vision of your why is not what your life looks like today. It is the blueprint of your future you are building now. You are creating it by starting with your imagination and belief.

Because repetition is so important for you to instill, and therefore believe, your vision, you must read your detailed why statement and picture your vision in your mind every day! Consume yourself with the vision of this realization throughout your day. As you do this, you are planting the reality and possibility into your being. Whether you speak of a small material item, such as a pair of pants, or a huge life event, like traveling the world with your soulmate, everything begins with a vision or dream in the spirit.

Because your why is the seed that must be planted before anything grows, the quality of the seed (the complete vision of the wish fulfilled) and the care given to it (repetition, faith, and emotion) are vital in the energy put into its realization. If this is where you put your first focus on before you go on to read about the skills for behavior change, just start with this. With repetition and faith—that you are worthy, that this is possible, that you are meant to expand— your vision will become more and more possible in your mind, body, and soul, and that is where it all starts.

**"The world says, 'Seeing is believing.'
Faith says, 'Believing is seeing.'"**

CHAPTER TWELVE

The Power of Goals and How the

Small Ones become the Big Ones

Did you get clear on a vision of a WHY? Could you feel the emotions of the fulfillment of your vision? Remember that this vision has the power to inspire change in you if you hold it close and clearly in your mind.

Once you identify your WHY for the change that you desire, it's time to now identify goals that will move you towards that vision.

There are different types of goals:

- Long term goals
- Short term goals
- Target behavior goals

Long term goals: These are goals or objectives that you want to accomplish in your future. Long term goals can take years to accomplish and are most often achieved through the successful completion of many short term goals. Long term goals can be very connected to your WHY vision, but are different. Long term goals can be desires stated as facts or future wishes. Your WHY can be your long term goal but emotionalized and visualized. For example, if your long term goal is to get healthier, your WHY would be your emotional connection to that goal. It would be the vision of yourself healthier, stronger, and happier. Your WHY connects your long term goal with belief and faith, and is more heartfelt than just a stated goal.

Examples of **long term goals**:

- Get healthy
- Become a competitive bodybuilder
- Learn a new language or skill
- Eat healthier foods and learn to cook
- Expand my social circle
- Write a book or develop a new program
- Become a millionaire
- Get a degree

Short Term goals: These are goals or behaviors that you want to accomplish in the near future or very soon, and are accomplished through the successful completion of target behavior goals.

Examples of **short term goals**:

- Drink more water
- Exercise regularly
- Sign up for a language class
- Eat more plants
- Get connected at school, church, in my community
- Spend time writing every week
- Save money every paycheck
- Find a job that I love

Target behavior goals: These are specific behaviors that are observable and measurable. These behaviors would be done on a regular basis, probably daily, as a planned and intentional action. These target behaviors, when done repeatedly over time, lead to new habits.

Examples of **target behavior goals**:

- Drink 64 ounces of water a day
- Go to my Pilates class on Mondays & Wednesday at 9am; Walk 2 miles with Sally on Tuesdays and Thursdays at 8am
- Attend Spanish class twice a week and listen to one Spanish podcast during the week
- Eat at least 4 servings of leafy greens a day
- Volunteer to chaperone the school dance this month
- Set aside time to write at 7am Monday - Friday for at least 10 minutes
- Put a minimum of $50 from my paycheck directly into my savings account every week
- Search for and apply for 3 jobs this week

Here is a format that shows these different goals side by side:

Long Term Goals	Short Term Goals	Target Behavior Goals
Get healthy and fit	Join a gym	Attend exercise classes 2x/week
		Walk around the block 2x/week
Become a millionaire	Save money and invest	Join an investor's group to learn strategies
		Save 10% money from every paycheck
Buy a home	Improve credit score	Pay all bills on time
		Pay down high credit card balances

It is important to identify your goals in all three areas so you know where you want to go and how you plan to get there. However, a long term goal, or even a short term goal, with no target behavior goal behind them are really just wishes. The simplicity of START with ONE will focus on the target behavior goals that will move you towards the realization of your short term and eventually long term goals.

We know that the simpler the target behavior is, the greater chance of you accomplishing it. And as small and as doable as these target behaviors are, done consistently, over time, they can produce massive results. The magic is in the daily behaviors. Look at how even the smallest of behaviors add up:

Done Daily	**=Weekly**	**=Monthly**	**=Yearly**	**Compound Results**
Save $2	$14.00	$60.00	$730.00	Dollars saved
Drink 40oz water	280	1200	14600	Water drank
Eat 3 servings of greens	21	90	1095	Servings consumed
Wake up 1 hour earlier	7	30	365	Hours added
Walk for 20 minutes	140	600	7300	Minutes walking
Read 5 pages	35	150	1825	Pages read
Say 5 affirmations	35	150	1825	Affirmations given
Meditate or sit quiet for 5 min	35	150	1825	Quiet minutes enjoyed
Say thank you to 3 people	21	90	1095	People thanked
Breathe deeply for 2 minutes	14	60	730	Present moments received
Take 20 stairs up to your office	140	600	7300	Stairs climbed

Everything we do, no matter how small, if done daily or very regularly, compounds for results. This goes in both directions - towards your goals, or away from them.

Toward Your Goals

- Instead of going to Starbucks in the morning, buy Starbucks coffee and make it at home and save around $975 a year making it yourself.
- Read 5 pages in an average book every day and at the end of a year, you will have read six books!
- Take that 20 minute walk every day and in a month you will have walked about 30 miles. In a year, you would've walked over 360 miles!
- Eat those three servings of greens a day and you will have taken care of ⅓ - ½ of your recommended daily fiber needs for the day.

Away from Your Goals

- In the other direction, eat a morning blueberry muffin from Costco at ~650 calories each, and you will have consumed almost 20,000 calories of muffins in just one month! Plus, you would be taking in almost double the amount of sugar grams recommended daily in this one muffin.
- Feed yourself or dwell in a worry, and you will likely be directing over 80% of your thinking on negative thoughts or experiences. That's up to 48,000 negative thoughts a day! That definitely adds up and it takes its toll on your body, mind, and spirit!

When we want to make positive change, we need to understand that small target behaviors have the power to create big change over time.

In the next chapter, I will outline a practical and easy way for you to identify one of those powerful but small target behaviors related to you and your goals so you can START with ONE right away. Then I'll give you tools and a structure to help support you towards success.

CHAPTER THIRTEEN

Get in G.E.A.R. Skills

This chapter is where the planning for physical action starts. By now, you have hopefully identified the state of health that you are in (Integrated Life Circle), what you WANT to create in your life, and you have your WHY vision in place. You should also have some self-awareness around some of your habitual behavior. After identifying where you are and where you want to be, the next step is identifying the HOW to change to bridge that gap. Here you'll learn practical skills that will guide you from the seed (idea) to the desire (emotions) to the actual creation (manifesting) of your desired results.

Let me introduce a method that will help you START with ONE small goal to begin your journey towards health. These **Get in G.E.A.R.** skills are designed to be the how-to of behavior change. They are as follows:

- **GOAL**
  - Establish a **target behavior goal** that is 100% achievable, specific, observable, and measurable, and keep track of your behavior.
- **ENVIRONMENT**
  - Organize and set up an **environment** that supports your goal behavior.

- **ASK for help**
  - **Ask** for the help you need to support, encourage, or motivate you in your target behavior goal.
- **REWARD**
  - **Reward** yourself for accomplishing your target behavior goal.

Using the Get in G.E.A.R. skills, we'll look at the *long term goal of eating healthier* and *learning to cook*. We'll identify our related *short term goal of eating more vegetables*. Then we'll START with ONE easy-to-incorporate *target behavior goal as follows*:

Target Behavior <u>GOAL</u> - I will eat 4 servings of leafy greens every day and 2 servings of other vegetables. I will keep track of my added vegetables in my food journal.

<u>ENVIRONMENT</u> - I will have cleaned and cut my leafy greens so they are ready to eat and add to my meals. I will wash and precut my other vegetables so they are ready to cook.

<u>ASK for help</u> - I will tell my family that these prepared greens are for meals and to prepare their own if they would like some. I will ask my partner to notice my commitment to my healthier eating and encourage me when he sees how well I am sticking to my behavior.

<u>REWARD</u> - I will put a big happy face on my food journal after I meet my target behavior goal.

Continuing with the Get in G.E.A.R. skills, we'll look at the *long term goal of experiencing more self-acceptance*. We'll identify our related *short term goal of exploring self*. Then we'll START with ONE easy-to-incorporate *target behavior goal as follows*:

Target Behavior <u>GOAL</u> - Prepare 5 easy-to-remember, kind, loving, self-acceptance affirmations and read or speak them to myself at least 10 times a day. As I say my daily affirmations, I put a check down so I can keep track and keep them in my intentional thoughts.

ENVIRONMENT - I will place my affirmations up on my mirrors, in my car, and on my refrigerator, reminding me that I am worthy of all good and wonderful things I am working towards, and that I have the power to create joy, love, and abundance in my life.

ASK for help - Tell my support people to remind me that I am beautiful and doing great if I start to feel small or negative about myself again.

REWARD - My reward will be more joy and a greater self acceptance of myself and my worthiness, believing that I am a wonderful, loving, and capable person.

And here is another example of using Get in G.E.A.R. skills for the *long term goal of writing a book.* We'll identify our related *short term goal of daily writing*. Then we'll START with ONE easy-to-incorporate *target behavior goal as follows*:

Target Behavior GOAL - Reserve the time of 8:00am to 8:30am Monday through Friday to write ideas, content, or outlines for my book. Put a checkmark on my calendar each day I write.

ENVIRONMENT - Keep my writing journal and tools on my desk and easy to see and access so I can start right where I left off. Put a "Do not disturb" sign on my door. Turn off my phone notifications.

ASK for help - Ask the people in the house to please not interrupt this dedicated writing time.

REWARD - My reward will be seeing my book unfold and develop, and feeling grateful and proud seeing my goal coming to life.

You will use the Get in G.E.A.R. skills to create your ONE small target behavior goal. It is the structure for you to use no matter what your long or short term goals are: wanting to lose weight, reduce stress, find a soulmate, or climb a mountain. Once you have identified what you want - long term or short term goals - you would START with ONE 100% achievable, specific, observable, and measurable target behavior goal, and support it with your new skills.

You would use your target behavior **GOAL** to guide your direction to identify ONE desired behavior, and you would keep track of it in writing to keep you accountable. Writing it down or tracking your target behavior in some way is super important! Tracking it will identify what you are actually doing (versus what you think you are doing). It will also give you information about any patterns that may be coming up if you are having challenges following through with your target behavior. Additionally, tracking will serve as a reminder to do your behavior because you will have a physical reminder.

You would then organize and set up your **ENVIRONMENT** to support your one behavior goal and do this in advance to make your new desired behavior easier to do, and your old, undesired behavior harder to do. Whether it's your kitchen, closet, office, or gym, you'll want to create an environment that reinforces you doing your target behavior. This could look like healthy food already prepared, gym clothes all packed, tennis shoes near the door, water bottle filled in your purse, positive podcast selected, auto deposit into your savings, etc.

The next step would be for you to identify and **ASK** for what you need to help motivate, encourage, and reinforce your healthy goal. This may be atta-girls, quiet time, walking buddies, phone calls, daily texts, or weekly accountability. Your support can come from co-workers, friends, or family. Select carefully and ask those whom you trust and who really want you to succeed.

And lastly you would **REWARD** yourself. This step literally has the power to rewire your brain. The law of effect states that when a behavior is rewarded, the behavior will be more likely to be repeated. Rewards are very personal and can be as small or easy as patting yourself on the back, smiling at yourself in the mirror with a positive affirmation, or a happy face on your calendar. It could also be a pedicure, massage, date out, shopping excursion, or fancy dinner. These rewards should be immediate or soon after you complete your behavior goal. Whatever it is, it should make you feel good, content, and happy with yourself.

Remember to START with ONE target behavior goal and make sure it is 100% achievable. If you feel like you should be able to exercise every day for 30 minutes, but only do 3 days for 20 minutes, you will feel like a failure and beat yourself up, AND you won't even appreciate the 60 minutes of exercise that you did do because you will feel mad or sad that you didn't reach your designated goal. That is not the way to change! You are trying to create a new habit /behavior and that takes time. The more achievable it is, the more successful you will be with the new behavior and the more likely you are to stick with it. If you adjust that target behavior goal to something that you KNOW you can do for sure, start there. That may be 2 times a week for 10-15 minutes. It may be 3 times a week for 8 minutes. Whatever it is, you want it to be achievable. If you find you are not reaching that target behavior goal, consider modifying it, then reinforce it with the other Get in G.E.A.R. skills:

You want to create success and confidence as you train your body and brain for a new habit. Be patient and kind to yourself if you don't make your goals. As needed, go back to your plan to see what you can do to fortify your structure using the Get in G.E.A.R. skills as your guide.

Know that these skills apply to any behavior change goal that you have: developing gratitude, enhancing focus, improving relationships, taking risks and getting out of your comfort zone, learning a new skill, or trying a new activity.

The Get in G.E.A.R. process helps identify target behavior goals and then gives you the structure to support these goals. And inherent in the process is the potential for greater awareness of your behaviors. It's only with awareness that we can choose because we can see there is another way. Where we only knew one way and it was so habitual and automatic, awareness lets us see another way, or maybe even many other ways.

The Crowd Out Method

The Crowd Out method is another awareness tool to use when you want to create healthier habits. The idea is, when you want to lose a bad habit, you crowd it out with a better, healthier habit in its place. In this way, you focus on what you want (new habit), and not on what you don't want (old habit). For example:

If you want to:	Crowd out with:
Drink less soda or caffeine	Drink more water or herbal tea

Stop partying so much	Take a night class, take up a new hobby, meet new people, learn a language, volunteer at a shelter, make a bucket list and plans to start checking it off

Reduce your screen time	Commit to reading a book, walking around the neighborhood, writing letters, prepping healthy food, planning a trip
Stop sitting around all day	Walk your dog, join a gym or an exercise class, find the outside stairs in your neighborhood and walk or run them, commit to finding a new walking trail every couple weeks, call your friends to walk with, take a dance class, join a gardening group, take up swimming or rowing, rent a bike, help a friend with their yard work.
Stop being so negative in my marriage	Write down all the good things about your spouse and think about these things with gratitude. Read this list daily. Tell your spouse daily one positive and uplifting thing about them or share your gratitude for them in your life. Plan a date to go play and laugh with your spouse.

Not be so lonely	Commit to smile at people when you meet them, even in passing. Try new things – take a class, join a church, hiking group, or singles mingle group. Start your day with 10 positive thoughts and connect them with gratitude, then deliberately share that feeling of gratitude with others. Give genuine compliments to people every day.
Stop wasting money	Write down all the necessities you have, then create a budget for those things. Open up a savings account and commit to saving all of the money in excess of your necessities. Allow yourself a small, predetermined allotment for pleasure and fun and stay committed to only spending that amount every month. Practice expressing gratitude for what you already have.

Pick just ONE thing and make a decision to DO something with it. If you want to get rid of a bad habit, think about ONE thing that you can add that would help CROWD out that one bad habit. Then, go through the Get in G.E.A.R. skills and pre-determine the what, where, how, and who to help support your new replacement behavior. If you just want to add in a good behavior (this will most likely naturally serve to crowd out something else) then do the same steps. The key is to pick ONE thing you want to work with. When you find success in that one thing, you add on. You are more likely to want to add on another behavior or more of what you are practicing when you have had success already.

"Note to Self: One in a row. Any success takes one in a row. Do one thing well, then another, then once more, over and over until the end, then its one in a row again."
Matthew Mcconaughey

Ask yourself these questions when you are walking through your Get in G.E.A.R. Skills plan:

- What specific target behavior **goal** can I do to move towards my short-term goal? Is this target behavior goal 100% realistic, specific, observable, and measurable? Can someone see me actually doing it? How is it measurable and how will I track my behavior? Miles, steps, calories, time, distance, pages, calls, meetings..?

- How can I organize and set up my **environment** to support my behavior goal? Prepping my food? Having my gym bag ready? Confirming my appointment? Meeting a friend? Paying ahead of time? Committing to a specific date? Placing affirmations and reminder cards around my home? Setting an alarm?

- What kind of support do I need to **ask** for, and who will I ask it from? What will help me when I feel tired, lonely, unmotivated, discouraged, or defeated? What energizes and encourages me to keep going? Who will I ask for help on a daily, weekly, or monthly basis? What does that support look and feel like? How can this person or group help me stay accountable to my goals?

- How will I immediately **reward** myself for good effort and reaching my target behavior goals? What makes me feel happy or accomplished? What would motivate me to keep going when the going gets tough? What would be a good reinforcement for me to keep wanting to accomplish my goals?

Use the Get in G.E.A.R. skills to create for yourself a plan to identify the behaviors that will move you to the fulfillment of your short term, then long term goals. Remember to keep it simple and START with ONE target behavior and then build from there.

"The secret of your success is found in your daily routine."
John C. Maxwell

Part V

DEEPER INTEGRATION

CHAPTER FOURTEEN

Environmental Effects

Because the idea of holistic or integrated health connects our entire being, I cannot leave out our connection to our natural environment and how our choices affect not only our health, but the health of others and our planet. Similar to our food situation here in the United States where chemicals that are known to harm our bodies are allowed in our food for all the reasons previously stated, so it is with our personal care products, cleaning supplies, air fresheners, pots and pans, plastics, weed killer, home goods, construction materials, nail care, and thousands of more products that infiltrate our home and work environments. These chemicals find their way into our bodies as we inhale them, absorb them into our blood through our skin, and ingest them. Tens of thousands of chemicals (~85,000) are in use in our environment in one way or another, and it's estimated that less than 1% of them have been tested on human health. [43]What we do know about the very small amounts of chemicals tested on human health is that many have shown links to illness and disease.

---

[43] Harvard University. New Toxic Substances Control Act: An End to the Wild West for Chemical Safety? By Cory Gerlach October 25, 2016
CNN Health. Everyday Chemicals May be Harming Kids, Panel told. October 26, 2010

In her book, CountDown, Shanna Swan, PhD, an award-winning scientist based at Mt. Sinai and one of the leading environmental and reproductive epidemiologists in the world, alerts us about the threats posed by hormone disrupting chemicals and our modern environment that are endangering reproductive health, fertility, and the fate of humankind. Swan says that following projections, sperm counts are set to reach zero in 2045. Dr. Swan blames "everywhere chemicals", found in plastics, cosmetics, and pesticides. These chemicals, such as phthalates and bisphenol-A (BPA) affect the endocrine system (the messaging system that controls and coordinates many of the body's functions and hormone system), disrupting our hormone balance and causing reproductive havoc. Basically Dr. Swan is saying that us humans are an endangered species if we don't correct this problem now.[44]

We do indeed have toxins all over our environment - in our food, air, water, home, and places of work. The question is not how you will escape the toxins in your environment. The question is how can you reduce the toxins in your environment. And there are many ways to do just that. Again, we come back to awareness. Once you are aware of the products you buy, use, or consume that have a higher toxic load, you can choose what and how you will continue their use, reduce their use, or get rid of them all together.

These widely used chemicals are found in our everyday environment and at some level, in all of the products listed above. These chemicals are known disruptors to our health. Among some of the health conditions related to these chemicals are: cancers, diabetes, Parkinson's disease, infertility, reproductive and developmental issues, disrupted liver, thyroid, and immune

---

[44] COUNT DOWN How Our Modern World Is Altering Male and Female Reproductive Development, Threatening Sperm Counts, and Imperiling the Future of the Human Race By Shanna H. Swan with Stacey Colino

function, decreased sperm count and penis size, low birth weight, and high cholesterol. Here's a short list of some of most commonly used chemicals wreaking havoc in our bodies and environment:

- Pesticides
- Phthalates
- Bisphenols (including BPA)
- PFAS chemicals (short for perfluoroalkyl and polyfluoroalkyl substances)
- Flame retardants

With the industrial age and the introduction of thousands of chemicals over the past 80+ years, our environment and everything in it, including us humans, are exposed to a barrage of chemicals - some not harmful to our health, and many others known to be harmful. It doesn't help that the agencies responsible for testing these chemicals and approving them for use are ineffectual and often powerless in their regulation ability. As an example, according to the Environment Working Group (EWG), there are around 10,000 chemicals approved to be used in the formations of personal care products. Of those 10,000, only 11 have been banned or restricted by the FDA (U.S. Food & Drug Administration). [45]In contrast, the European Union has banned or restricted 1400 chemicals from personal care products, and Canada over 600.[46] As a nation, the consumer protections in this area, and many other areas, are feeble and weak.

But when we know better, we can do better. The government, nor the big companies being allowed to formulate with known toxic

---

[45] Environmental Working Group (EWG). The Toxic Twelve Chemicals and Contaminants in Cosmetics, By Scott Faber. May 5, 2020

[46] Safe 'N" Beautiful. European vs US and Canada Cosmetics Regulations. A World Apart. Feb 11 2022

ingredients, will be coming to the rescue of this issue anytime soon. It is you and I who must demand change. We do this with our vote. Our most powerful vote is with our wallet - in what we choose to buy or not to buy. It is basic supply and demand. If the demand ends for chemical-laden shampoos, makeups, baby toys, foods, plastics, cleaning supplies, air fresheners, fabrics, and the endless list of other daily used products on every shelf in our markets, then the supply ends. If demand for cleaner and safer products goes up, so does the supply.

If this connects with you and you want to START with ONE thing to help you reduce your toxic load or the toxics in or around your home and family, consider one of these changes below. Once you adopt and connect with one small change, you can add another, and then another. You can slowly but surely reduce your exposure to these chemicals one decision at a time.

- Buy organic when you can (Refer to EWG's Dirty Dozen and Clean 15 list when shopping. Ref in Resources)
- Eat different kinds of produce to avoid potentially high exposure to a single pesticide.
- Minimize exposure by avoiding plastic food containers and never reheat food in plastic
- Use glass instead of plastic
- Check product labels - avoid anything with "fragrance" or phthalates listed
- Keep dust levels down in your house by wet mopping and vacuuming with a HEPA filter
- Wash your hands before eating since hand-to-hand contact can lead to flame retardant exposure
- Avoid buying furniture and baby products filled with polyurethane foam
- Cut down on canned foods and don't microwave food in plastic containers or cans

- Avoid plastics with a 3 or 7 recycle code on the bottom and use non-plastic containers when possible for food or drink
- Choose BPA-free water and baby bottles
- Eliminate or reduce use of candles, air fresheners, and perfumes or fragrances in your home–
- Use the Environmental Working Group's (EWG) Guide to Healthy Cleaning to get a grade on the cleaning products you are using and/or you may want to switch to. Stick with the Verified, A, and B ratings for the safest products. www.ewg.or/guides/cleaners
- Get the EWG Skin Deep app to look up your personal care products, or search for them on the web and then put "EWG" after the product and find it's rating. www.ewg.org/skindeep
- Consider going clean with the products that you use everyday that stay on your skin, such as serums, moisturizers, and makeup. (As a clean beauty advocate for Beautycounter, I know that their commitment to educate, formulate, and advocate for cleaner products is unparalleled. They do this while simultaneously creating extremely high-performing products.)
- Get a good water filter in your house, whether it's a pitcher filter, on or under your sinks, or a whole-house filter.
- Bring your own bags to the grocery store
- Ditch the coffee lids on to-go cups
- Use a reusable water bottle
- Use bees-wax covers instead of plastic wrap
- Buy cleaning detergents in a box
- Use wool balls in the dryer to control static cling instead of dryer sheets
- Reuse glass jars as food containers
- Learn how to recycle, then do it!

- Buy local as much as you can, especially local farmer's markets (this also has you buying in-season and fresh)
- Open your windows for ~10-15 minutes a day to bring in fresh air and circulate the air in your home.
- Get a home air purifier or get air purifying plants.

Keep it very simple and don't feel like you need to change everything at once. The things we buy and use all the time are habits, and just like any other habit, we START with ONE small thing to change at a time. As your awareness expands, you will see many more small ways that you can make healthy changes to your body, home, and environment. START with ONE easy thing to replace or get rid of and go from there!

CHAPTER FIFTEEN

Stick with It!

"It doesn't matter if you fall down, it's whether you get back up."
Michael Jordan

It's often been said that it takes 21 days to form a new habit. That may be true for some. But considering a habit is something that is repeated over and over again until it becomes basically unconscious or automatic, it may take much longer than 3 weeks to incorporate a new habit. I have heard it takes between 21 days and 200 days to incorporate a new behavior and turn it into a new habit. The truth is, it will take what it takes, and the more you repeat the targeted behavior and instill it with an immediate reward, the quicker you will establish a habit around it. Changing our habits takes awareness, time, and directed effort. It takes patience and grace too, because it is almost certain, at some point, that you will fall, forget, or fail in your new behavior. THAT is part of the learning, the growing, the discovery of self. It isn't failure unless we miss the opportunity to learn from it. If you expect, plan for, and have an open attitude towards these 'learning opportunities', you can change these "failures" into wonderful lessons that will expand your thinking, your compassion, and your resilience.

My karate instructor used to tell us that the only difference between a white belt and a black belt was that the black belt never quit. This is the truth. Sometimes when you can't show up fully, just show up – as you are – and know that in that moment, that is enough. Sometimes we can't show up with our A game, or even our B game. Sometimes, it is all we can do to just not quit. And in that moment, that's okay, because this too shall pass.

But keep the faith in yourself, even when it gets hard or doubt creeps in. Know that making healthy change doesn't require one to be specially skilled, intelligent, resourced, or connected. It does take a desire to make a decision, to create the thoughts and thereby the actions to change, and the support of a plan and a structure to lean into. Anyone can change and create a better life for themselves. Anyone.

Always go back to the idea that you can START with ONE!

Figure out what you want - what you really want - then START with ONE! Get in G.E.A.R. with one target behavior *goal* that is supported with an *environment* that makes your behavior easier, *ask* for the support you need, and decide on a *reward* that reinforces your success.

Recommit daily to your target behavior goal. Write it down and read it first thing in the morning, throughout your day, and before you go to bed to imprint your vision in your mind.

Every time you read your goal, visualize yourself already succeeding and feel the emotion that comes with that vision of success.

Speak only affirmative and kind words to yourself - words that assert that you got this, and that no matter if or how long you are down, that you can get back and create the thoughts, habits, and therefore, the life that you want to create.

And remember that information alone is not power: information WITH action is power!

"There are far, far better things ahead than any we leave behind."
C.S. Lewis

Conclusion

I congratulate you for taking the time to read this book. I hope and pray that you practice whatever skill, message, or piece of information that spoke to you, and that you trust the process of starting with ONE thing to begin a movement towards loving self-care and better integrated health.

As you move into the direction of awareness, awakening, and change - one action at a time - you will feel more power over yourself, your thoughts, and your behavior. With this awareness, you will begin to see things that you don't see now. It is the evolution of our growing and becoming. You can gladly and lovingly accept where you are right in this moment, and trust that definite movement in the direction of health and abundance is underway.

And always remember grace. It covers all your pains and errors as you learn and grow and become. Perfection is never the goal, as there is no such thing here. It is the messy, broken, and trying soul wanting to expand that is so perfectly beautiful.

I am so often overwhelmed with this grace - this love. It is in this love that I find my WHY. My love for people, the planet, myself, and God. It is my love to share this hopeful message that you can create true health in your life. It is from this place that I wrote this book. Thank you for the privilege to speak to you. This book has been a collaboration of my experience, my passions, my gifts, and God's leading in my life. I am honored for the opportunity to create this!

May you share the hope and practicability of this idea with others, leading them with your inspiring acts of your ONE thing, that led to two, to three, to something new in your life. Keep growing, my friend. Remember, you do not ever sit still - nothing does. You are in movement whether you believe it or not. Your part in the movement is deciding which direction you will move - towards fullness and health, or towards decrease and death.

I hope you choose life.

Resources

Dr. Frank Lipman, MD Functional Medicine.	https://drfranklipman.com/
Dr. Hyman is a practicing family physician and an internationally recognized leader, speaker, educator, and advocate in the field of Functional Medicine.	https://drhyman.com/
EWG's Dirty Dozen & Clean Fifteen – a list with the dirtiest (highest residue of pesticides) fruits and vegetables, and a list of the cleanest (least amount of residue).	Ewg.org
Food Activist Vani Hari, better known as "The Food Babe."	https://foodbabe.com/
Health Activist Robyn Obrien	https://robynobrien.com/
Oxford Happiness Questionaire:	http://www.meaningandhappiness.com/oxford-happiness-questionnaire/214/

NUTRITIONFACTS.ORG is a science-based nonprofit organization founded by Michael Greger, M.D. FACLM, that provides free updates on the latest in nutrition.	https://nutritionfacts.org/about/
Pesticide Action Network check it out to see what pesticide residue is found on everyday foods	https://whatsonmyfood.org/
Zach Bush MD a physician specializing in internal medicine, endocrinology, and hospice care:	https://zachbushmd.com/

MEAL KIT DELIVERY SERVICES
https://www.greenchef.com/
https://www.purplecarrot.com/
https://www.sakara.com/
https://www.sunbasket.com/

BOOKS

10-Day Detox Diet	Mark Hyman, MD
As a Man Thinketh	James Allen
Atomic Habits	James Clear
Change your Paradigm, Change your Life	Bob Proctor
Fiber Fueled	Will Bulsiewicz, MD, MSCI
How to Be Well	Frank Lipman, MD
The 5 Second Rule	Mel Robbins
The Four Agreements	Don Miguel Ruiz
The Power is Within You	Louise Hay
The Power of Awareness	Neville Goddard
The Rain Barrel Effect	Stephen Cabral
Think & Grow Rich!	Napoleon Hill
Wallace D. Wattles Trilogy	Wallace D. Wattles
Wishes Fulfilled	Wayne Dyer

PANTRY FOODS TO HAVE ON-HAND

Apple cider vinegar	No-salt-added peanut or almond butter
Red wine vinegar	Old-fashioned rolled oats
Baking powder and baking soda	Olives or capers
Balsamic or sherry vinegar	Pure vanilla extract
Beans: cannellini, navy, chickpeas or black	Raw almonds, cashews, walnuts
Brown rice and Long-grain white rice	Seeds: sunflower, flax, chia or hemp, sesame
Chicken broth	Salsa
Coffee	Salt: sea salt or kosher salt
Dried fruit: raisins, apricots or cherries	Spices: Rosemary, Oregano, Bay leaves, Curry powder, crushed red peppers, Chile powder, ground Cinnamon, cloves, cumin, ginger, nutmeg, granulated garlic
Eggs	Tea
Extra virgin olive oil	Tomato paste
Flour: all purpose, whole wheat or pastry	Tuna
Garlic and onions	Unsweetened plain soy, oat or almond milk
Grains: bulgur, quinoa, couscous or farro	Whole grain pasta
Honey	Whole grains
Lentils	

REFRIGERATOR FOODS TO HAVE ON-HAND

Vegetables	Salsa
Fruits	Hummus
Greens	Eggs
Fresh Herbs	Garlic & Ginger
Dates & dried fruits	Frozen Vegetables & Fruits
Nuts & Seeds	Frozen meats or plant-based proteins
Plant-based milks	Tortillas

https://www.forksoverknives.com/wellness/22-healthy-foods-to-stock-fridge/

FOR MORE RESOURCES FROM
KATHLEEN KLUG, VISIT:

kathleenklugbook.com

No matter your goal — whether you want to improve physically, mentally, emotionally or spiritually — you will have the tools, structure, understanding and support to improve, restore and integrate your health and create more energy, joy and purpose in your life! When you have health — true integrated health — you can create and do just about anything! Having this kind of health is everything, and you are the one that must take charge of your health. Be your own champion in your own life and START with ONE, right now!

Learn More About Kathleen

Kathleen Klug has been working with people as a Fitness & Health Professional for more than 40 years and is very passionate about teaching and encouraging people to be their very best and most powerful selves. Kathleen is here to inspire, inform, motivate and walk alongside you on your journey to revitalizing your health and wellness!

kathleenklug.com

START with ONE E-COURSE BY KATHLEEN

Enroll in Kathleen's Start With One (SWO) e-course and gain access to 9 self-paced modules that walk you through the SWO process of your Integrated Life Circle, The State of your Health, the "Power to Heal" chapters and so much more! You will learn how to identify your long-term, short-term and target behavior goals, and then how to apply them with the "Get in G.E.A.R." skills!

START TODAY AT KATHLEENKLUGBOOK.COM/COURSE

6-WEEK GROUP COACHING SESSIONS

You can begin your START with ONE journey now!

Join a SWO 6-week group with Kathleen to jumpstart your health journey with direction, accountability and inspiration alongside the support of others along the way!

FOR MORE INFORMATION ON GROUP OR INDIVIDUAL COACHING, OR TO SIGN UP, VISIT KATHLEENKLUG.COM.